INTERPOL

INTERPOL

The Inside Story
of the International
Crime-Fighting Organization

Michael Fooner

Henry Regnery Company ● Chicago

Library of Congress Cataloging in Publication Data

Fooner, Michael.
 Interpol.

 1. International Criminal Police Organization.
HV7240.I25F66   364.12'06'11   72-11172

Contents

1
The View
from Saint-Cloud

On a clear day the view of Paris from the suburb of Saint-Cloud is breathtaking. At the foot of a steep slope the river Seine throws a gleaming coil around the Bois de Boulogne. Beyond the river the city stretches to the edge of the sky. Sacre Coeur, the Eiffel Tower, Notre Dame—the familiar landmarks catch the eye as it wanders over the endless prospect of cupolas, skylights, and gables.

There is one spot in Saint-Cloud from which the view is even more remarkable. Rue Armengaud is a quiet street lined for the most part with one- and two-story private residences, each with its sloping, gabled roof. Towering above them is Number 26, eight stories high, a long, contemporary structure of glass, steel, and stone with a fifty-foot slender metal rod sprouting from its incongruously flat roof. From Number 26 the view extends far beyond Paris to Berlin and Vienna, to London, Rome, and Stockholm, to Nairobi and Rio de Janeiro and Buenos Aires, to Montreal, and to Washington,

1

D.C. The people of Number 26 who enjoy this unique view also enjoy unique powers of communication, for through the metal rod above their heads they talk to the police of the world and the police of the world talk to them.

Number 26 is the home of the International Criminal Police Organization, known to police forces, criminals, and police buffs everywhere as Interpol. To millions of readers who avidly follow the annals of international crime in the daily and periodical press, the name Interpol conveys a special thrill. Their appetite for the excitement and melodrama that they believe accompanies the pursuit and apprehension of criminals is especially whetted by a particular kind of crime story that appears from time to time in their favorite newspapers, a story that usually reads something like this:

INTERNATIONAL CON MAN CAUGHT;
INTERPOL SCORES AGAIN

Donald Martin, alias Armand Esterhazy, alias René Tronter, alias Estaban Villarejo, came to the end of his long, smooth-talking road yesterday in Bombay, where the relentless arm of the law finally caught up with him.

Martin, who took off from Kennedy Airport six months ago, blazed a trail of duplicity from New York to London to Paris to Wiesbaden to Tel Aviv and finally to Beirut that netted him over three-quarters of a million dollars. Posing either as a Belgian businessman called Tronter or as Corporate Executive Señor Villarejo from Buenos Aires and occasionally using his American name, Martin conned dozens of importers into writing orders for commodities from crude rubber to machine tools. Armed with a passport to match each change of identity, he obtained money in each city through a variety of deceptions.

Police along his route became aware of his activities as protests from fleeced merchants began reaching their headquarters. Then the lines of international communication with Interpol began to hum.

Checking their master file, a twenty-foot-long rotary card

index, Interpol sleuths concluded that Martin, Tronter, and Villarejo were all the same man. Though his photo and fingerprints were lacking for positive identification, one Interpol agent had his memory jogged by a description of the con man's old-world mannerisms and quaint pince-nez. A further check into the master file produced a description that seemed to match —that of a Hungarian swindler named Esterhazy who was brought to Interpol's attention some years ago in connection with an American case. The agent placed a call to the FBI in Washington, D.C., and learned that an Esterhazy had immigrated to the United States in 1953, had been naturalized, had a criminal record, and had changed his name to Martin.

Now armed with a set of Martin's fingerprints, Interpol sent out an IPCQ alert (Interpol Paris to all national bureaus) warning member police forces to be on the lookout. The national bureau in India passed the message to all domestic metropolitan police forces. An airport stakeout spotted Martin as he alighted in Bombay. He was Mr. Tronter on the passenger list, but on the ground he was just another flabbergasted crook when he walked into the hands of the police at the passport checkout counter.

"I can't understand how this happened. I moved so fast!" he said to his captors.

"Interpol moves faster," he was told as he was led away to a detention cell.

Martin faces extradition proceedings that could keep him backtracking to the penal accommodations of every country in which he has been doing business.

The story has all the elements of a major motion picture: colorful international locales; an ingenious, smooth-talking crook using old-world charm to relieve stuffy business types of their hard-earned cash; police of five countries baffled by the false trails he has left behind him; an international superpolice organization with a fantastically efficient system at first unable to pin him down, then moving swiftly, finding the clue that leads to the solution of the case; the transatlantic call to the

FBI; a coded bulletin flashed to police on the other side of the globe; the apprehension of the criminal just before his moment of final success. A film with such a plot could give millions of law-abiding moviegoers the impression that this is the way international criminals are caught, that there is an international crime-fighting organization whose agents come up with instant solutions to apprehend criminals who practice on an international scale.

So much for fiction. Most people are aware that, besides such spectacular arrests, there are other crimes conducted on an international scale, such as drug traffic, in which the crooks may escape detection for years and enjoy their profits. People know that arrests are made and criminal enterprises halted, but international crime seems like an octopus with its arms constantly in motion, too large and too many for more than amputations here and there, and they wonder what effect this has relative to the whole beast. Some people also are aware that there is indeed an international crime-fighting organization called Interpol, but its workings, and the workings of international crime, are infinitely more complex than described in our fictitious journalistic account, imperatively more subtle than the fictitious portrayals of recent television programs and motion pictures.

In the layman's mind, the name Interpol probably conjures up a "Man from U.N.C.L.E." vision of a worldwide force of secret agents aided by a staff of beautiful people, operating hidden laboratories and arcane files that supply instant solutions to the most baffling crimes. In actuality, Interpol agents do not patrol the world. They never make arrests, nor do they engage in shoot-outs. Interpol's people are hardworking, open persons employed for their skills, and the organization itself is not a huge switchboard plugged into an information-retrieval system. It may be noted in passing that the idea of a European crime squad has been advanced at various times, and each time it has foundered. Many legal and political considerations make such an organization extremely difficult if not impossible to realize. Too many questions without suitable answers arise; too many problems lacking solutions become apparent. For instance, where would such a squad get its judicial powers? How would longstanding rivalries between local, regional, and national police agencies be resolved? Would these rivalries be intensified with a superpolice agency on the scene? Is it practical to assume that an international system of legislation for the functioning of such a superpolice force could be established in our lifetime?

The Benelux countries, Belgium, Luxembourg, and the Netherlands, have in a sense adopted the supranational crime squad idea with their treaty on extradition and mutual assistance in criminal matters, but it is far short of the ideal. Their arrangement provides for the delegation of an investigation assignment by the police of one cosignatory country to the police of another for the purpose of continuing an investigation. It makes for continuity of tracking a suspect from any one of the three countries into another on a routine basis if the suspect is liable to extradition. In an emergency, it makes possible the direct arrest of a suspect by police of one country up to ten kilometers inside foreign territory. It took five years to get the three Benelux countries to ratify this modest effort at direct international police work; getting all the European nations to agree to a comparable arrangement would seem to require an incalculable amount of time, given present feelings about national sovereignty.

The truth about Interpol is actually far more exciting than any fiction. Behind the dossiers and detection techniques is the most interesting crime detection device of all, the mind and spirit of man. The story of how man's search for a truly workable method of coming to grips with crime and the criminal brought Interpol into being must be told if one is to understand the nature of this unique institution.

The idea that eventually brought forth Interpol can be said

to have been born after a gestation period of over a hundred years. Its origins may be said to have been previsioned in a trend of emerging police science that began in the early years of the nineteenth century. By the closing years of that century this trend was paired with a sociopsychological impetus that was felt throughout Europe, an impetus to find something entirely different from the punitive systems of criminal justice inherited from the past.

In a sense, every system of criminal justice is founded on correct identification of a criminal and his crime. Historically, the methods by which society identifies its criminals have been of profound importance and great variety. Nations have relied on methods ranging from the supernatural, as exemplified by the mark of Cain in Biblical times, to denunciations and torture in the feudal age, to the human genius of gifted investigators during the Era of the Great Detectives in the nineteenth century, to the contemporary adulation of computer technology.

The means by which a society deals with the problem of criminal detection conditions its process of law enforcement and its system of criminal justice, and that, in turn, is one of the foundations of the quality of life in that society; to the extent that the foundation is faulty, the structure of the law and the penal code attendant on it not only fail to protect society, but may also encourage the growth of crime.

The evolution of Interpol represents an effort of nations to deal with this problem by acting in concert. A large segment of its work deals with methods for identifying offenders, assembling comprehensive information about them and making it available to law-enforcement officials throughout the world.

The annals of police science suggest that this concept originated among the police of Paris more than a century and a half ago, during Napoleonic times, when the city was struck by a crime wave of intolerable proportions.

In 1809 a certain Baron Pasquier, the prefect of Paris

police, took action. Ingeniously, he acquired the services of a criminal. François Vidocq, born into a poor Parisian family in 1775, began his life as a criminal and paid for his crimes with a term in prison. Under the prefect's patronage and protection, Vidocq created a special detective bureau. In effect, the baron set a thief to catch other thieves.

Vidocq was the best possible choice for the job. Not only was he familiar with the leading and lesser figures in the French underworld, but he also possessed a phenomenal encyclopedic memory for faces, which enabled him to finger and correctly identify any one of a host of robbers, murderers, embezzlers, thieves, burglars, and fences. Vidocq went even further. He recruited the most capable of his former associates to the cause of the law, trained them in their new assignment, and formed them into a disciplined corps of undercover operatives. They successfully kept tabs on the activities of the criminals of Paris and also kept an all-seeing eye on the influx of apprentices as they joined the ranks of the professionals.

During the twenty-three years that Vidocq was in charge of this operation, his bureau became known as the Sûreté. At constant odds with most of his colleagues, who had come to police work with more conventional backgrounds, he was removed from office in 1833, accused of instigating a crime for the purpose of uncovering it. By that time he and his men had developed a formidably efficient technique for collecting and storing information regarding each known criminal. When the bureau began its operations, and for some years after, Vidocq's men had to rely principally on their memories. Each man carried in his head his own personal information-retrieval system in which he filed away for instant reference scores of individual bits of data concerning the physical characteristics and habits of each criminal with whom he was familiar. To this he added the results of his observations and experiences from day to day. As the original group of criminals-turned-detectives grew old and died or retired and as the number of criminals increased, the system became unwieldy. Newcomers to the force had to undergo a rigorous apprenticeship and learn all the minutiae that the old-timers had carried in their heads, to which they were then expected to add their own contributions as they became familiar with criminals on their own.

Vidocq replaced this personal memory system with one of written files, or dossiers. A file was started in the name of each criminal who was brought to the attention of the bureau. In it were kept a written description of his physical appearance, a detailed description of whatever peculiarities of speech, manner, or dress he exhibited, a careful description of his modus operandi, a drawing of his face, and, after the advent of photography in the 1840s, a mug shot.

The system was a major advance in the history of police work. Based on Vidocq's systematic method of identifying offenders, the Paris police became the acknowledged leaders of the world in law enforcement. Visitors to Paris are said to have been astonished at the speed and efficiency with which fugitives from the law in their native countries were arrested when they got to Paris.

Unfortunately, the dossier system carried within itself the seed of its own failure. The Paris police became such enthusiastic record-keepers that within five or six decades they had produced an enormous archive that required maintenance by an army of clerks. Mountains of records piled up in the dusty, gaslit halls of the prefecture until, with five million dossiers on file, it took an incredible amount of time to locate and pull the ones that were wanted.

The system, which had been noted for its efficiency in the heyday of its creator, became a nightmare of inefficiency and remained so until another genius appeared on the scene. His name was Alphonse Bertillon, a clerk in the criminal records office of the Sûreté. In 1879 Bertillon came up with an original system for keeping records on people in trouble with the police. His system was based on the classification of bodily measurements and characteristics. An outgrowth of the then fledgling science of anthropology, it was, like most startlingly new ideas, ridiculed and rejected. Bertillon persisted, however, and after the prefect's job had changed hands several times and a more sympathetic administration was in office, he had a chance to prove his system. On February 20, 1883, through his measurement system, he was able to unmask a suspect who was using a false name and who claimed never to have been arrested before. Bertillon was roundly applauded and had the satisfaction of seeing his application of the science of anthropometry, dubbed "bertillonage," put into immediate use by the Sûreté.

Bertillonage was adopted by the police of several other countries as well, and it might have become one of the fundamental contributions to criminology had not another and more certain system superseded it. Even as Bertillon was winning acceptance, two other men, unknown to each other and to Bertillon, were laying the foundations for a method that soon would render bertillonage outmoded.

The story of the origins and acceptance of fingerprint identification strongly resembles that of the theory of evolution. In 1859 both Charles Darwin and A. R. Wallace had independently come up with exactly the same conclusions based on remarkably similar observations. In 1877 a British civil servant in India named William Hershel decided after years of study that the human fingerprint could be used for positive identification and suggested to the inspector general of prisons in Bengal that he use such a method to keep track of the prison population and to track down fugitives from justice. The idea was rejected out of hand. In the meantime in Japan, a Scottish physician, Henry Foulds, had noticed that Japanese artists made a practice of pressing their inked thumbs against their works as a means of identification. Giving the matter some study and thought, Foulds came to the conclusion that the pattern of each person's fingerprint was unique. In 1880 he wrote a letter to the editor of *Nature*, the noted English scientific journal, suggesting that fingerprints could be used to identify criminals. The letter was published, and Hershel, upon reading it, wrote immediately to the magazine, asserting his own claim as the originator of the idea.

The ensuing controversy between Hershel and Foulds came to the attention of Sir Francis Galton, the father of the science of eugenics. Galton, a familiar figure on the lecture circuits and a talented dilettante in certain scientific areas, had become sufficiently interested in Bertillon's system during the early 1880s to experiment with it and to lecture on it. When the Foulds-Hershel controversy broke out, he began to include a discussion of fingerprinting in his lectures. Eventually Galton became so enthusiastic over the possibilities that he wrote a book on the subject in 1892 and pressured Scotland Yard to adopt fingerprinting as a means of keeping tabs on England's criminal population.

The two systems of criminal identification, bertillonage and fingerprinting, battled for police acceptance until the latter finally prevailed around the world. Bertillonage continues in principle as the basis of a specialized identification system applied to photographs at Interpol. The significance of the two methods lies in the important principle that was being born. Both systems were founded on the same concept—a universal system of personal identification—making it possible for the first time in the annals of police work to bridge linguistic, geographical, and cultural barriers between the police forces of different countries. A common "language" was being established for identifying society's adversary, the criminal.

In 1893 a German criminologist, Franz von Liszt, who held the chair in criminology at Berlin University, pointed out that criminals were showing a remarkable ability to roam the world at will and that consequently the police were losing track of them. Liszt expressed his views shortly after Galton's book on fingerprinting was published. In 1904 the French police became concerned over the growth of the white slave traffic. Young women were being lured from their homes, ostensibly to join dancing troupes, and were finding themselves in the brothels of Marseille, Cairo, and Buenos Aires. The French proposed that other countries equally concerned join them in establishing some sort of central office that would make possible international cooperation in combatting this evil.

At first the appeal fell on deaf ears. In 1910 the French tried again, this time calling for a convention of broader scope that would attempt to deal with other criminal offenses in addition to white slavery. The response was negligible, but the pressure for some such movement was now building. Prince Albert I of Monaco took up the cause. He had previously shown an interest in the subject of justice when he attempted to intervene in the Dreyfus affair. Finally there convened in Monte Carlo at his invitation an international meeting of jurists, lawyers, and police officials from twenty-four nations with Brazil, Cuba, and Guatemala representing the Americas. Presiding over the meeting was the dean of the law faculty of the University of Paris. All the conferees were in agreement. Some sort of international effort was necessary to combat international crime. The delegates went home pledged to work to that end. The year was 1914. Within a few weeks after the meeting had adjourned most of Europe was at war. The pledges made at Monte Carlo had to be shelved.

Ideas are hard to kill, however. Somehow, like the roses of Picardy, the concept of international cooperation among police forces survived the barrages and the trenches, and in 1923 the call to organize went out again. This time there were positive results. An international police organization was about to be born.

2
Birth and Rebirth

I_N 1923 Dr. Johann Schober, police commissioner of Vienna, revived the idea of an international police organization. A man of great prestige, impressive in appearance and possessed of a dynamic personality, Schober had been chancellor of Austria in 1921–22 and would be chancellor again in 1929–30. As police chief of one of Europe's principal cities, he was vitally aware of the need for international police action in postwar Europe. The Austro-Hungarian Empire had been dismembered, and new states had been carved out of the old map of Europe. Each state was independently printing bank notes. Placed against the background of chaos that inevitably follows any political cataclysm, the situation made Europe of the twenties a happy hunting ground for forgers, swindlers, and black marketeers. Taking advantage of the general disruption, they moved about easily from country to country.

13

Perhaps the existence of the newly formed League of Nations helped provide the proper atmosphere; whatever the reason, Schober's invitations brought together 130 delegates from 20 countries. Their objective was to form an association for mutual assistance and systematic cooperation built on the ideological foundations that had been laid nine years earlier in Monaco. The First International Criminal Police Congress of 1914 had given top priority to the development of methods for the quick exchange of information on international criminals and to the improvement of procedures for arresting them and returning them to the country in which they could be tried. These goals were reaffirmed in 1923. In fact, the 1923 meeting was intended as much as possible to carry on where the 1914 meeting had left off. With an eye to history, Schober called his meeting the Second International Criminal Police Congress. Most of what had been decided in Monaco under French leadership was reaffirmed before the delegates moved ahead to create an International Criminal Police Commission, the organization that evolved into Interpol. It was decided to have headquarters in Vienna and to have the police commissioner of Vienna automatically serve as president. That was to prove a fateful decision, though no one could have foreseen it at the time.

Making an Austrian head of the organization was no mere gesture. There were at least two sound, practical reasons for doing so. The Austrian police for years had maintained excellent records on international criminals—a good starting point for the new organization. Moreover, at a time when most European countries were preoccupied with their own badly tangled financial and commercial affairs, Austria alone was willing to provide a home and working facilities despite its own slender financial reserves.

Membership in the commission was on a national basis. Each member nation paid into a general fund one Swiss franc for every ten thousand of its inhabitants. New members simply filed notice of intent to join, paid their subscriptions, and were automatically placed on the roster. By 1939 every European country except the Soviet Union had joined, as had a number of American and Asian nations. The United States joined in 1938, in time to be on the scene for the organization's temporary demise, an event that will be covered in greater detail in a subsequent chapter.

Quite naturally, Austrians filled most of the posts on the executive committee. Dr. D. O. Dressler, a lawyer and chief of the Austrian Federal Police, became the secretary general, a post he was to hold until 1939. A more fitting candidate would have been hard to find, for Dressler spoke and wrote French, Italian, Spanish, English, and German with enviable fluency. Schober, the commission's guiding light, served as its first president. A General Assembly rounded out the organization's administrative echelon.

Originally the commission had been established under the joint jurisdiction of the international congress that had brought it into being and Austria, the host nation. General membership meetings were held annually. In 1930 the General Assembly voted to declare the commission independent of the congress and to elect its officers by majority vote. Gradually, as the commission organized its own departments, it became increasingly independent of Austrian domination as well. Unfortunately, as we shall see, the commission did not cut the umbilical cord completely.

From the start it was generally understood that the International Criminal Police Commission, or ICPC, was not to be a working police force. Police officers of one country cannot at will carry on their activities within the national boundaries of any other country. The commission established its functions with complete respect for national sovereignty. It served as an information center and exchange for its members and asked member nations for the quick arrest of criminals pending extradition proceedings. One cardinal rule was observed as closely as it is today. The commission's members pledged themselves to an exclusive concern with common criminals and not with political, racial, or religious matters. Eventually, as the commission expanded its activities and the organization grew, the central bureau in Vienna also concerned itself with international search warrants, forged documents, counterfeiting, and drug smuggling.

By 1930 the commission headquarters in Vienna had assembled a secretariat of its own with specialized departments that included a Central International Bureau, which dealt with counterfeiting in all its aspects; an International Criminal Records Office; a bureau that collected fingerprints and mug shots; a bureau that concerned itself with passport forgery; and a monthly periodical called *International Public Security*, which was printed in French and English. By 1935 an international radio network was started to provide the police of member nations with their own fast, far-reaching communications system that would grow ultimately to circle the globe. Simultaneously, the national police authorities of member nations were establishing special units for international criminal records.

But also in 1935 the international stage was becoming obscured by sinister shadows. The commission's General Assembly that year was held in Copenhagen. The German delegate was General Daluege, a young, arrogant Nazi whose only qualification to head his country's police was, he laughingly declared, that he had been an inmate of almost every cell in Berlin's Moabit Prison during the years of the Weimar Republic. The General Assembly was described by the late Harry Söderman, who was present as a delegate from Sweden, in his autobiography, *Policeman's Lot*. According to him, Daluege was physically huge and wore the light green uniform of a police general. His contributions to the proceedings seem to have been driving around Copenhagen in a two-hundred-horsepower sports model Mercedes and challenging Söderman to a drinking contest that Daluege lost. Daluege never reappeared at subsequent conventions. His place at the assembly was taken first by Arthur Nebe, then by Carlos Zindel. Söderman described them both as professional policemen and "very mild Nazis" who lost their political orientation as time went on. Nebe attended as head of the German criminal investigation division and was eventually executed for taking part in the conspiracy to assassinate Adolph Hitler. Zindel was destined to play a special role in the revival of the International Criminal Police Commission after the fall of the Third Reich.

The assembly's annual meetings from 1935 until the beginning of World War II were increasingly marked by the severe strain the German presence placed on the organization as a whole. The strain built up from year to year until it reached crisis proportions in 1938. Earlier that year, Austria had suffered the German *Anschluss*, and Vienna had fallen from the status of the capital of a sovereign nation to that of a German provincial town. Schober had died long before this, in 1932. He had been succeeded by Police Commissioner Skubl, who was ousted and replaced by an Austrian Nazi named Steinhausl as soon as the Nazis marched in. True to the qualifications that the Nazis seemed to demand of their police chiefs, Steinhausl had spent some time in prison. In fact, he had been in a penitentiary cell at the time of the *Anschluss* and went almost directly from his cell to his post as head of the city's police force. This was a serious blow to the ICPC, for under its constitution Steinhausl was automatically its president.

The 1938 assembly, the last convened by the International Criminal Police Commission before World War II, was held in Bucharest. During the opening sessions, the Germans began a campaign to take over not only the proceedings but the organization as well. Because of Austria's absorption into the Greater Reich, many of the delegates wanted to move the headquarters out of Vienna. Heinrich Heydrich, who was by then chief of German police, proposed that since Austria was now part of Germany and since the chief of the Vienna police had always been the commission's president, that post should now be held by the director of the Sicherheitspolizei—in other words, himself.

Tension at these meetings must have been all but unbearable, for by the end of the first week a special effort had to be made to hold the organization together. The Romanian hosts invited the delegates to take a break and relax on the royal yacht for a cruise down the Danube to the Black Sea. Söderman devotes several paragraphs in his autobiography to a description of that cruise, using it to illustrate the lengths to which the commission went at this particular time in its attempts to nurture good personal relationships through socializing among the police chiefs of member nations. Each annual meeting was held in the capital of one of the members, giving the host nation and city an opportunity to go all-out in providing not only the usual convention facilities but also entertainment, which sometimes reached sumptuous proportions. Perhaps the Romanians outdid everyone else, due to the unusual circumstances surrounding the 1938 convention. This occasion must have seemed to delegates—accustomed as many of them were to the normally austere life style of a police official—like a Roman emperor's orgy.

The passengers on that idyllic voyage consumed Russian caviar by the ton, drank a Niagara of champagne, and enjoyed troupes of gypsy singers and dancers, a free twenty-four-hour bar, and two orchestras. They were showered with everything that had made the capitals of *Mitteleuropa* a byword for glamor and gracious living before Hitler's booted legions goose-stepped them under. Söderman's description of that Danube cruise reflects the scandalized lift of the eyebrows with which the hardworking police officials on it must have recalled the event in later years. He describes evenings when the yacht dropped anchor at fishing villages along the river to

Birth and Rebirth   19

be greeted and serenaded by hundreds of fishermen who sur-
rounded the ship in small boats, each adorned with a paper
lantern, each fisherman strumming a mandolin. There were
folk dances, moonlight flirtations between delegates and
gypsies, and friendly rivalries for the ladies' favors. General
Marinescu, the Romanian chief of police, occupied a special
suite of staterooms, which he shared with a beautiful secretary
whose husband was forced to sleep in bachelor quarters just
above the keel. According to Söderman, the mood of the
cruise was one of "agreeable madness."

When the yacht reached the Black Sea, the delegates were
provided with fishing gear. Those who were able, given the
rigors of their marathon partygoing, fished for sturgeon,
hoping perhaps to keep the caviar in good supply—not that
there ever seemed any danger of its running out despite the
high rate of consumption. The delegates sailed back up the
Danube and proceeded to Belgrade, filled, presumably, with
Gemütlichkeit equal to the champagne they had consumed.
Their tensions relieved, they wound up the business of the assembly and departed for their native countries, vowing to
meet the following year in Berlin. Ostensibly, the differences
between them had been resolved, at least for the time being,
but the next year never arrived for the commission.

In August, 1939, before that year's annual meeting,
Heydrich proposed that the commission move its headquarters
to Berlin and insisted that the members vote on the proposal
through the mails. He gave the delegates three weeks to
respond. In September, long before the three-week period was
up, Germany invaded Poland. When, in view of the international situation, many of the delegates did not bother to mail
in their votes, their silence was all too readily taken by the
Germans as acquiescence. Within a matter of weeks after the
outbreak of hostilities, Heydrich had the organization's files
and records moved to Berlin. By the spring of 1940 German
panzers were advancing deep into France and Belgium,

German paratroopers were dropping onto Holland, Denmark, and Norway, and Italy was attacking France. All of Europe was embroiled. In 1941 Heydrich, who was chief of the newly united police of all Germany and therefore chief police commissioner of Vienna, named himself president of the commission. He was, in effect, president of practically nothing. Little remained of the organization. Though the Germans kept the commission going as a kind of window-dressing operation, Söderman felt that they did not use it for their own political purposes. Marcel Sicot, former secretary general of Interpol, says they didn't because they couldn't—the organization and its files were geared otherwise. According to Söderman, the commission still retained some value even during the darkest hours of the Nazi night. Through its offices, it was possible for neutral members to help some of their colleagues escape the consequences of German occupation. Söderman's book cites the case of Kristian Welhaven, police commissioner of Oslo, who was arrested by the Germans during the occupation of Norway. He was first sent to a concentration camp, where he was put at hard labor, and then to a cell in the infamous Gestapo prison cellar in Berlin. With the ICPC acting as intermediary, Söderman says that Swedish efforts to save him were successful. Welhaven was released from his cell and sent into exile in a Bavarian village, where his wife was allowed to join him. He remained there until the end of the war, when he resumed his duties in his native country.

Heydrich took over a villa, probably from a non-Aryan, in the fashionable Berlin suburb of Wannsee and used it to store the commission's files. The villa was also the scene of a historic meeting between Gestapo Chief Ernst Kaltenbrunner and Count Folke von Bernadotte at which the count tried to negotiate the release of concentration camp inmates. It was in this same villa that the Gestapo made its headquarters when their building in Berlin was destroyed by Allied bombs. Eventually the relentless bombing reached Wannsee. The villa was hit, and most of the ICPC files were destroyed.

As the war came to an end in Europe and the final scenes were played out in Berlin streets and at Hitler's bunker, Carlos Zindel performed his final service to the spirit of international police cooperation. As the Russians fought their way into the heart of the city, he left Berlin in his car, drove to Wannsee, placed what remained of the commission's files in the back seat, and drove to French military headquarters in Stuttgart. There he handed over the files and attempted to give himself up. The French accepted the files but, according to Söderman, treated Zindel disdainfully and told him to come back at a more convenient hour. He was then head of the German criminal investigation division and a Nazi only for the sake of political convenience. Zindel must have taken this insult as a final blow to all that he had left—his professional pride. He went into a nearby park, sat down on a bench, and swallowed potassium cyanide. His last living action ultimately provided a nucleus of files when Interpol was revived. Their value became apparent within a very short time as it became increasingly evident how many prewar criminals had survived the rigors of war.

There is some difference of opinion among researchers as to who was the prime mover in the reestablishment of Interpol in 1946. Florent Louwage of Belgium is usually credited with having taken the initiative. Undoubtedly the idea came to several minds at once, for a large number of ICPC officers and delegates were alive and actively functioning as policemen when the war ended. At any rate, in that year several of the prewar Interpol officials, including Louwage, inspector general of Belgian police; Harry Söderman of the Swedish Criminological Institute; Werner Müller, chief of the Swiss Federal Police; Louis Ducloux, director of service of the French Judicial Police; and Ronald Howe, assistant commissioner of

Scotland Yard, met in Brussels. They formed an executive committee, issued invitations, and were soon joined by delegates from nineteen nations, all intent on reestablishing an international police organization. The ICPC, which seemed to have perished with the Nazi takeover and the war, was found to be alive and well and ready to open shop again.

3
Laying
the Foundations

THE summons to Brussels brought responses from a majority of the original members of the International Criminal Police Commission.

Söderman makes some interesting statements in his book concerning the personalities and circumstances that attended this rebirth. He describes Florent Louwage as the only prominent member of the old commission who, in his words, "had come untainted out of the ordeal," meaning the war—a remark replete with inferences.

He also notes that the Polish delegates, a colonel and a major, were partisan officers who had been made police officers, that the colonel was seven feet tall and the major only five feet, making them the Don Quixote and Sancho Panza of the gathering. None of the Russian satellite countries continued its membership for very long after the first meeting, nor have any reinstated themselves at this writing. However, the Soviet Union, Poland, Czechoslovakia, and Romania do

23

subscribe to the Geneva Convention on Currency Counterfeiting, which is administered by Interpol.

The criminals with whom the ICPC had been concerned
were very much in evidence. Many of the prewar international
swindlers, forgers, and con men were back in business, if
indeed they had ever been out of business. The old games between criminals and police resumed as though the war had
never occurred. There was one difference: the "bad guys" had
become older, and their lined faces and gray temples were not
so easy to identify from the old mug files.

The first order of business was to revive the old commission. As if to memorialize the sense of continuity that per-
vaded the air in Brussels, the 1946 meeting was subsequently
entered on Interpol's official list of General Assembly annual
meetings as the fifteenth. It was eight years since the four-
teenth, to be sure, but the intent was unmistakable. The torch
was being carried forward.

Some things remained as they had been—the requirements
for membership, the constitution, and the bylaws, for instance,
and the intent of the organization to maintain and promote international cooperation among criminal police authorities.
Other things had changed under the hammer blows of history,
and new questions had to be considered—the matter of a permanent headquarters, for instance. Since Austria was under
four-power occupation, Vienna could not again become the
headquarters city, and the members decided to look elsewhere. A contest developed between the Belgian and
Czechoslovakian delegates, each contending that the
headquarters should be established in his respective country.
Because the commission had been central European in its orientation before the war, the Czech's claim had a certain
weight. The Belgians, however, pressed their claim, and the
debate became deadlocked. Although the founders of the organization were determinedly apolitical, the debate began to
sound like a reflection of the East-West division that was soon
to become the Cold War. Before a split could develop in the

membership, however, a compromise was arranged, and France was offered the honor of housing the headquarters.

The reasons for this choice were persuasive. French police had an excellent reputation for internationalism in outlook and working cooperation. Historically, they had been in the forefront of the movement to establish international cooperation for the suppression of crime. Now they were willing to undertake the financial and other obligations that would inevitably accompany the honor of being the ICPC headquarters nation. Louis Ducloux, the ranking police official in the French delegation, conferred with his country's minister of justice and got permission to accept. Thus international police cooperation "came home" to France forty years after its officials had first proposed the organization of a central office for the purpose.

The choice of France as the commission's headquarters meant under the rules of the old commission that the secretary general would automatically be French. The position was offered to Ducloux. Louis Ducloux was a popular figure among his fellow police officers both at home and abroad. He had had a brilliant career in the Sûreté Nationale, beginning as an inspector and working his way up, step by step, to the summit of the French police hierarchy. His official title was director of service of the Judicial Police, the French counterpart of the CID.

Since he wished to retain his position even while he served the commission, Ducloux accepted the commission's offer with the proviso that the Sûreté would supply him with an assistant who could act as his deputy. A rising career officer, Jean Nepote, was named deputy and eventually became secretary general in his own right some years later. Today, a number of national police organizations that belong to Interpol contribute to its manpower by assigning officers to tours of duty at its headquarters. These men retain their pay and seniority rights and return home with specialized training in international crime work.

The matter of the headquarters settled, the new commission proceeded to revive the General Secretariat and the Central International Bureau, both of which were to be headquartered in Paris permanently. Mindful of Heydrich's seizure of the presidency under prewar commission rules, the commission decided to make the presidency an elective office and to open eligibility to delegates from all member nations. They also decided to establish an executive board of five consisting of the president, the secretary general, and three reporters general. Florent Louwage became the organization's first president. The other three positions were filled by Ronald Howe of Scotland Yard, Werner Müller of the Swiss Federal Police, and Harry Söderman of the Swedish Criminological Institute.

Marcel Sicot, the secretary general after Ducloux, wrote a book entitled *A la barre de l'Interpol*. In it he describes Florent Louwage as a dynamic person, small, delicate, dark-complexioned with "funny eyes," alert, and friendly. Sicot writes that though Louwage's health was not the best, he was endowed with nerves of steel and had enormous reserves of energy. He began his career as an ordinary bureaucrat low on the totem pole of the Belgian police and quickly built for himself a brilliant career through his interest in public affairs. Sicot also writes of Louwage's love for the concept of authority, which he sometimes conveyed to the world at large in his staccato voice. He spoke English with a heavy Flemish accent, delighting his Anglo-American friends and colleagues.

The old name, the International Criminal Police Commission, along with its postwar constitution and bylaws, stayed with the organization until the annual meeting of the General Assembly in 1956 in Vienna. The delegates then decided that the word *commission* carried a connotation that suggested a temporary body. Their aim was to create a public image of permanency for the organization, the kind of image that would reflect creditably on its status in the growing community of international bodies. The remedy was simple enough. The General Assembly voted to change the name from *commission* to *organization*, paralleling other major multinational agencies, beginning with the United Nations Organization.

The curious appellation "Interpol" was also acquired at about this period. Credit for it goes to Dr. Giuseppe Dosi, a delegate to the ICPC and then head of the Italian Interpol bureau. A dynamic man, short and stocky in stature, with a ready wit, Dosi proposed the name at the Vienna General Assembly, and his fellow delegates agreed. As to its origins, Marcel Sicot tells the following story.

He and Dosi were touring Italian police installations. As they went from place to place, they held press conferences publicizing the international organization. At the time, ICPC radio units had been using the organization's cable address as part of their on-the-air signature: "This is Radio Interpol calling."

Up to this time the world press had not paid a great deal of attention to ICPC. Aware of this and perhaps trying deliberately to remedy the situation, Dosi and Sicot made frequent references to the ICPC radio sign-off during their press conferences. Reporters began to pick up the word *Interpol* and use it in their stories. The label caught on and spread across Europe and to the United States, where it had the dubious distinction of appearing in the title of a fictional television series, "The Man from Interpol."

A formal resolution was proposed at the Vienna meeting, approved, and written into Article 1 of the new constitution adopted at that meeting: "The Organization called the INTERNATIONAL CRIMINAL POLICE COMMISSION, shall henceforth be entitled The INTERNATIONAL CRIMINAL POLICE ORGANIZATION (INTERPOL)." Vienna, the birthplace of the old commission, was also the scene of its metamorphosis into the new Interpol.

Interpol's constitution, its general regulations, and its financial regulations were modeled on those of other international organizations such as UNESCO, the Universal Postal Union, and the World Meteorological Organization. Article 2 announces the organization's aims, one of which is "to ensure and promote the widest possible mutual assistance between all criminal police authorities within the limits of the laws existing in the different countries and in the spirit of the Universal Declaration of Human Rights." The reference to what is commonly called the International Bill of Rights affirms Interpol's concern with more than simple "law and order." It indicates a dedication to the larger commitments of human dignity and social well-being. Another aim is "to establish and develop all institutions likely to contribute effectively to the prevention and suppression of common law crimes."

Article 3, like some of the other articles in the new constitution, is a restatement of the letter and spirit of the old commission's philosophy and intent: "It is strictly forbidden for the Organization to undertake any intervention or activities of a political, military, religious or racial character." This feature of the Interpol constitution is also an essential guideline for the day-to-day handling of major crime problems. Criminal activity frequently impinges on the political sphere. A given crime, such as a bank robbery, can be purely criminal, or it can be simultaneously criminal and political—if the bank is robbed by a revolutionary organization to finance its political activities, for example. The originators of international police cooperation recognized that the organization would be unable to function or survive if it became involved in situations that were even vaguely political or that were related to military, religious, or racial matters.

Sometimes this prohibition has to be weighed and applied with the utmost delicacy, especially if the crime is large in scope and outrageous to the public. Such a situation arose in the late 1960s when aircraft hijacking—or "skyjacking," to use the term coined at the time—began to occur worldwide and with disturbing frequency.

Here was a crime that seemed uniquely within the purview of Interpol, since virtually all skyjackings were on international flights. Yet it quickly became apparent that the organization would have to move with circumspection, since most of the perpetrators asserted political motivations for their actions.

Nations whose airlines were being victimized and whose nationals were being jeopardized turned promptly and persistently to Interpol for help in combatting the growing crime wave of the skies, especially since joint action was obviously essential if the problem were to be dealt with. While skyjacking was not precisely a new kind of crime, its increase in the late sixties was remarkable, and it was obvious that Interpol was uniquely equipped to rapidly assemble techniques and facilities to combat it.

In September, 1967, at the General Assembly in Kyoto, and again in October, 1968, at the General Assembly in Tehran, demands were made that Interpol take action. At the same time members expressed concern about the political overtones. These at first did not seem very compelling to the public. Aircraft were being hijacked mainly by individuals who were alienated from society or who, suffering from personal aberrations or emotional instability, asserted that they had political motives. But soon skyjackings were being engineered by conspiratorial organizations bent on harassment of or rebellion against established governments. The majority of members were wary of opening the way for controversies that might split Interpol along ideological or national lines.

But Interpol could not ignore a problem of international crime that was so prominent and so much a matter of public concern. Most distressing of all was the apparent helplessness of national police and the victimized airlines. At this juncture Interpol moved firmly but discreetly. First it prepared a study of the problem that could serve as a guide to all nations on preventive and punitive measures. It then made the results of its study available to certain international organizations with which it had special relationships—the International Civil Aviation Organization (ICAO), the United Nations General Assembly, and the International Air Transport Association (IATA).

Since the members of those organizations all had full access to their own national police agencies, coordinated efforts against skyjackers were now possible, including the technical expertise assembled by Interpol. At the same time it was a matter of record that Interpol had completely refrained from looking into the political aspects of the question and had acted strictly and correctly within the terms of its constitution.

Feelings ran high, especially as the seriousness of the offenses increased from simple diversions of aircraft to seizures for ransom, bombings, and destruction by explosives. Some nations proposed that the subject be brought up for debate at General Assembly meetings in 1969 at Mexico City, but the majority rejected the proposal, preferring to let other organizations take action—organizations that had a direct concern and with which Interpol maintained relationships. The ICAO and the IATA became vehicles for international cooperation against this form of crime, and ultimately special multinational conferences were convened by countries directly concerned. The threat of a split in Interpol over this touchy subject was dispelled at the General Assembly in 1970 in Brussels with a unanimous vote that all member nations work through the two air transportation organizations.

In 1972, however, the group was moved by events to agree that Interpol should use its facilities to help combat such forms of international criminality as hijacking and terrorism. Several landmark resolutions were passed unanimously. Skyjacking was declared to be a common criminal offense even if the perpetrator claimed political motives, and the same principle was applied to other terror tactics such as sending letter-bombs through the international mails. Still, Interpol's constitutional prohibition against concern with political matters was reaffirmed. Now, however, Interpol headquarters would be authorized to obtain and circulate information on crimes of these kinds, act to prevent them, and distribute wanted notices on perpetrators. National bureaus were authorized to cooperate in tracking down and apprehending such terrorists and blackmailers.

Another problem that Interpol has had to solve is the relative influence of the various member nations of the organization. Under Article 4 of the Interpol Constitution, membership is open to official police bodies delegated by their countries as members, but only if their functions come within the framework of the activities of Interpol. This obviously excludes police organizations that deal in political matters, either internal or international, including espionage and counter espionage. Requests for membership are submitted to the secretary general and are subject to approval by a two-thirds majority of the General Assembly.

International organizations always face the possibility of a takeover by a particular country or bloc of countries that may try to use them for their own purposes. Members are usually very sensitive to such a possibility and act promptly whenever such an attempt is suspected. Witness the complaints made by opposing blocs of nations within the United Nations almost from its inception. Eastern bloc countries have complained for years that the Western bloc, and the United States in particular, has dominated the Security Council and the General Assembly. Recently the shoe seems to be on the other foot, and the United States, Great Britain, and other Western nations have complained that the assembly has been taken over by delegations from Asia and Africa.

That such a thing should happen to an international police organization is unthinkable; indeed, it is highly unlikely that the organization could exist should such a takeover occur. Article 30 of the Interpol Constitution forbids the secretary general or any of his staff to solicit or accept instructions from any government or authority other than Interpol itself. It further instructs every member nation to respect the international character of the secretary general and the Secretariat and enjoins members from trying to influence them in the performance of their duties.

Article 41 made it possible for Interpol to establish relations with intergovernmental or nongovernmental international organizations concerned with problems that also concern Interpol—narcotics, counterfeiting, skyjacking, and so on. Through this article, Interpol was able to establish relations with the Customs Cooperation Council, the European Committee on Crime Problems, and the United Nations Commission on Narcotic Drugs and Economic and Social Council.

When this new constitution came into force, on June 13, 1956, the membership comprised the national police organizations of fifty-seven nations. Included were the police of two geographic entities—the Saar and the Netherlands Antilles—that, strictly speaking, were not countries but were considered to have status that qualified them for membership. The Netherlands Antilles continues on the membership rolls to the present; the Saar does not. In 1956 the countries represented in Interpol were Argentina, Australia, Austria, Belgium, Brazil, Burma, Cambodia, Canada, Ceylon, Chile, Colombia, Costa Rica, Cuba, Denmark, the Dominican Republic, Egypt, Eire, Finland, France, the Federal German Republic, the United Kingdom of Great Britain and Northern Ireland, Greece, Guatemala, India, Indonesia, Iran, Israel, Italy, Japan, Jordan, Lebanon, Liberia, Libya, Luxembourg, Mexico, Monaco, the Netherlands, the Netherlands Antilles, New Zealand, Norway, Pakistan, the Philippines, Portugal, the Saar, Saudi Arabia, Spain, Sudan, Surinam, Sweden, Switzerland, Syria, Thailand, Turkey, the United States of America, Uruguay, Venezuela, and Yugoslavia.

The United States was listed as being represented on the membership roll, but its participation seemed ambiguous for a time. Later on its interest revived, and it became one of the most active members.

Since then the proliferation of new nations, particularly in Africa, Asia, and the Pacific, has been reflected in Interpol's expanding membership list. Ten years after the new constitution came into force it reached the one-hundred-member mark, and by 1971 the annual meeting of the General Assembly in Ottawa admitted the one hundred and eleventh member to a roster that ranged through the alphabet from Algeria to Zambia.

That was the year in which Interpol finally attained "legitimacy." Even though by 1971 it had been operating for nearly half a century, its legal status had not been clearly defined. Its long search for clear legal status may seem like nothing more than a curiosity in the annals of international organizations, but the lack of such status meant that there was always a serious possibility of its being challenged, hampered, or thwarted in its work. While the question of legitimacy could be considered mainly theoretical, there were many practical problems that hinged on the question of Interpol's identity among international bodies, problems affecting collaboration with other organizations, taxes, and potential lawsuits.

In 1966 the secretary general, Jean Nepote, had submitted to the membership a report on the organization's legal status that described the anomalies of the situation. He noted that, although Interpol was recognized throughout the world as an international agency, although it employed at the time over ninety people permanently in its General Secretariat, and although hundreds of police officers in affiliated countries worked with it in their national central bureaus, although it had an annual international budget of two million Swiss francs and owned real estate (its headquarters building) and movable goods (radio and photographic equipment, office furnishings, and so on) worth some eight million Swiss francs, and although it was mentioned by name in many international agreements and engaged in daily pursuits that often resulted in certain persons losing their liberty, nevertheless, the legal basis of its existence could be subject to challenge.

As Nepote pointed out, by 1966 the "hierarchy" of international organizations and their legal status were clearly established. By and large the organizations fell into four major categories: the United Nations, the supreme international body; specialized U.N. agencies such as the United Nations Educational, Scientific, and Cultural Organization, the International Labor Organization, the Food and Agriculture Organization, and so on; some two hundred ordinary intergovernmental organizations that are independent of the United Nations—the International Bureau of Weights and Measures and the International Coffee Organization, for example—which were brought into being by conventions or treaties signed at diplomatic levels and binding on governments that supported them financially; and well over a thousand nongovernmental organizations created by private parties, either individuals or corporations, for nonprofit purposes, and having no official character and no connection with any government.

Interpol fitted into *none* of these categories in the *de jure* sense. It was not one of the United Nations' specialized agencies; it was not founded on a convention and therefore was not considered to be an intergovernmental organization; and it did not have intergovernmental status. Its members were neither individuals nor associations; they were official police bodies that took part in the organization's activities, although without direct and continuous instruction from their governments.

In fact, in 1958 the Council of Europe had said of Interpol, "The legal status of the ICPO-Interpol does not place it in any well defined category of agencies for international cooperation; clearly it is not a nongovernmental organization."

However, the United Nations had given Interpol consultative status, though not immediately upon its reorganization. A request for such status had been submitted to the world body in April, 1947, and had been denied because Interpol was thought not to have nongovernmental character. A second request, however, filed in 1948, had explained more clearly the organization's nongovernmental character, and consultative status had been granted. Thus Interpol took its first important step toward some measure of *de jure* legal status.

Though the *de jure* situation was decidedly not favorable for full legal status, the *de facto* situation was more promising. The first recognition of legal status for Interpol had come six years after it was established and had to do with one of the most prevalent areas of international criminal activity. As noted earlier, the emergence of new nations after 1918 brought an upsurge in currency counterfeiting.

The old countries were just as vulnerable. The problem assumed such alarming proportions that in 1926 the League of Nations was asked to intervene. A committee set up by the league studied the problem and presented to the parent body in 1929 a report that has since become known as the Geneva Convention on Currency Counterfeiting. It was signed by the representatives of twenty-six countries and is still in effect today. (Oddly, the United States, which has the most serious counterfeiting problem on an international scale, is not a signatory as of this writing.)

The Geneva Convention contained twenty-nine articles establishing the principles by which the cooperating governments were to attempt to suppress counterfeiting. One principle stated that the counterfeiting of the currency of any country would be considered a crime punishable in any other country in which the criminal was apprehended. The convention clearly named the following as crimes: making counterfeit currency, carrying it into another country, and uttering it (the legal term for putting it into circulation).

This was an important event in the annals of international police work; the signatory nations had agreed that anyone committing a particular crime in one country would be treated as an offender in other countries and would be apprehended and returned to the country whose laws he had broken.

Just as important from Interpol's viewpoint was the final act of the Currency Convention, which recommended that, "pending the creation of an international office . . . the work of the International Bureau of Vienna [today Interpol's General Secretariat] which was fully appreciated by the Conference, should be continued with the completest possible cooperation of the Governments; according to the information supplied to the Conference, the International Bureau, by centralizing information as to counterfeiting currency, displays an activity which is directed to the task which might be alloted to the organization contemplated in Article 15."

The convention also called for the periodic convening of currency counterfeiting conferences, and the first was held on March 9, 1931. At this conference, it was recommended that the Central International Bureau of the ICPC should pursue the work of centralizing information on currency counterfeiting in liaison with the national central bureau in each country that had been set up under the terms of the convention to deal with the problem. It was also recommended that the ICPC take over publication and distribution of the specialized publication called *Counterfeits and Forgeries Review*, first published in 1923 by the police of Vienna. This was another major step forward for Interpol. Though the League of Nations had sponsored the currency convention, the league had no machinery to implement the convention. It therefore turned to the then recently formed ICPC, which was ready, willing, and able to undertake the administration and enforcement of the convention. Ever since, Interpol has maintained specialized bureaus to investigate and suppress counterfeiting activities.

Further *de facto* recognition came in 1947, when the International Telecommunication Union, during a meeting in Atlantic City, appended to its International Telecommunication Convention a paragraph that specified that the frequencies needed for the international exchange of information for the purposes of the arrest of offenders would be selected, by agreements between the agencies involved, from the frequency bands set aside for fixed antenna broadcasting. Since Interpol administers the only operative international police radio network, it has since then acted on the paragraph and is in constant contact with the ITU in Geneva.

And in 1955 the United Nations Commission on Narcotic Drugs adopted a resolution that "exchanges of information on the illicit traffic should be effected by the quickest possible means and . . . that for this purpose the competent authorities should make use of the machinery for cooperation elaborated by the ICPC." When the Commission on Narcotic Drugs met thereafter, it regularly invited an observer from Interpol who, *de facto*, enjoyed the same rights as observers from intergovernmental organizations.

The Council of Europe, after deciding that Interpol was not a nongovernmental organization, signed an agreement of cooperation with it in the form of an exchange of letters, thus recognizing Interpol as having status equal to that of the specialized agencies of the United Nations. Furthermore, several European international conventions on extradition, legal cooperation, and the like have explicitly provided a role for Interpol in the implementation of international procedures.

Several nations have done much to enhance Interpol's *de facto* legal status. Most of the countries affiliated with it have solemnized their accession in a document signed by the chief of state or by an appropriate minister, and many countries have confirmed their affiliation by law or decree; for instance, the United States passed such a law on July 22, 1958; Argentina issued a decree on January 22, 1962; Morocco issued a decree on June 30, 1962; and Bolivia issued a decree on April 19, 1962. In addition, delegates to Interpol's General Assembly are appointed by appropriate government authorities in all affiliated countries; credits and facilities for Interpol cooperation are allocated in official texts or orders; the organization's financial needs are accounted for by contributions that appear in national budgets approved by parliamentary bodies in affiliated countries (these are regular commitments and are regularly paid); and many members of governments make public statements about their government's participation in the work of the organization.

Ironically, the question of Interpol's *de facto* legal status was thorniest in its host country, France. In that country, if a corporate body is to enjoy the fundamental right of holding property, its existence must be officially recognized. Interpol's General Secretariat building, constructed at a cost of many millions of Swiss francs, is a most palpable piece of property situated in a suburb of Paris. International organizations obtain official recognition in one of two ways: either by signing an *accord de siège* with the French government—actually an international treaty between the French government and those other governments that are represented by the organization—or, when a nongovernmental organization is involved, by meeting requirements set forth in a law passed in 1901. This law states that an association is an agreement in which several persons pool resources for an end other than profit-sharing; that any such association wishing to obtain legal status must be made public by its founder; that no foreign association can be formed or can function in France without the prior authorization of the minister of the interior; that all groups that have the characteristics of associations, and have their headquarters in France, and are administered by foreign nationals shall be considered foreign associations.

Clearly, Interpol did not fit into the category of an association under the terms of the law of 1901. In fact, had Interpol admitted that this law did apply, it would have had to submit itself to the approval of the French minister of the interior and would have declared itself to be a private association. The first was unthinkable in view of the nature of Interpol's work and affiliations, and the second was simply not true. Nepote noted in his 1966 report that, strictly speaking, Interpol had no formal *de jure* legal status in France. Agreeing, the French Finance Ministry said as much in a letter to him in July, 1963, that concerned the granting of certain forms of assistance for the construction of Interpol's headquarters building. The question came up in regard to Interpol's application for certain tax exemptions and in regard to the contracts it had negotiated. Neither the request for exemption nor the contracts appeared to have any legal status in France.

Nevertheless, Interpol had in actuality been transacting its daily business for twenty years. It had a bank account in Paris and a post office checking account; it hired personnel for whom it paid regular contributions to the French health insurance program; and it had signed a lease and other contracts.

The French parliament seemed to recognize Interpol's legal existence when it passed Article 11 to Finance Law No. 63-779 on July 7, 1963. It stated that "the Minister of Finance is authorized to grant up to limits of 3 and 4 million francs respectively, an official guarantee for the loans contracted by the International Civil Aviation Organization and the International Criminal Police Organization for the construction of administrative buildings."

Although this article was positive, Interpol's legal position was precarious in its headquarters country, despite the fact that it undoubtedly had a *de facto* position and was an international public service with all the attributes of an intergovernmental body except that of a founding convention. Nevertheless, evidence of many governments' confidence can be found in the *de facto* arrangements mentioned thus far.

This legal maze may seem of little account for all practical purposes. A close examination of Interpol's actual early legal position, however, turns up several embarrassing facts that had to be considered.

First, since it was not officially recognized as an intergovernmental organization as far as the United Nations was concerned, Interpol was lumped in with the mass of some one thousand nongovernmental organizations. According to Nepote, this could have been severely damaging to its prestige and international authority, particularly with respect to international associations of police officers, which are nongovernmental and legally exist on the same basis as Interpol. This could have hampered Interpol's efforts to oppose any attempt to encroach on its powers and prerogatives.

Second, because of its unclear legal status, the organization had to handle a number of ordinarily routine matters in a somewhat indirect manner. For instance, when Interpol wanted to obtain for its Secretariat employees the social benefits to which they were entitled under French law—a pension plan, health insurance—the employees had to be entered on the organization's books as employees of the *International Criminal Police Review*, a periodical that the organization publishes and distributes to its members.

Third, Interpol might have incurred criticism in performing certain of its basic functions. For instance, individuals might have challenged the organization's right to broadcast their descriptions worldwide and might have attempted to prevent the information from being used against them. Employees who suffered accidents while traveling might have had difficulty in obtaining reimbursement for doctors' bills or for medical treatments. Another organization could have infringed on Interpol's vital interests in such a way as to involve it in litigation, upon which, as the owner of considerable assets, Interpol would have found itself obliged to go to court to defend itself and its rights.

The best solution was for Interpol to be "intergovernmentalized," as Nepote put it in his report, through its United Nations relationships. In the interim he negotiated a headquarters agreement with the French government that recognized Interpol's *de jure* status. The agreement also granted Interpol the means to carry out the tasks for which it had been organized and granted it certain privileges such as the rights to sign contracts, to buy and sell property, to defend itself in court, and to enjoy diplomatic privileges for its headquarters; the exemption of its property from seizure, confiscation, or expropriation; freedom regarding the possession of foreign currency; exemption from direct taxation of property or real estate purchases; and exemption from customs duties on equipment. This kind of agreement usually was signed by the French government only with intergovernmental organizations.

In September, 1971, Secretary General Nepote was able to announce that, by special arrangement with the United Nations Economic and Social Council, Interpol's consultative status was replaced by a new and special arrangement granting it the status of an intergovernmental organization.

Under this arrangement, Interpol, the United Nations Secretariat, and the Economic and Social Council agreed to exchange all appropriate information and documentation on matters of mutual interest; consult at the request of either party on matters of common interest; collaborate in the study of such matters and establish technical cooperation in substantive projects; send observers to each other's meetings that deal with matters of common interest and that are relevant to the work of those bodies; propose items for each other's provisional agendas.

The agreement was on the agenda of the September, 1971, session of the General Assembly in Ottawa. Nepote, answering fears expressed by Panamanian and Indian delegates, stated that the agreement would in no way alter the organization's principle of noninterference in political matters. The agreement was approved unanimously. Interpol's legal status as an international crime-fighting organization was clarified.

Indeed, it is difficult to imagine how Interpol had been able to operate so successfully for so long without being subject to serious legal challenges. Interpol has continually transacted business without going through the usual diplomatic channels, for crime and criminals do not wait for diplomatic niceties. The object has been to bypass protocol and formality when necessary in order to counter crime without impinging on national sovereignty. When one recalls that the smallest international matter is seldom accomplished without months or years of prior arrangements, Interpol's uniqueness in this regard is notable.

Through the years, Interpol has shown an ability to adapt and grow. Its constitution calls for the General Assembly to meet once a year, each time in a different city. Until 1960 Interpol's assembly met exclusively in European countries, a reflection of its European origins. In 1960 the "continental barrier" was broken, and the assembly met for the first time outside Europe—in Washington, D.C.

The break was a response to the irresistible flow of world events. Interpol's major new growth had been taking place in all parts of the globe. A criticism that was often heard both inside and outside the organization was that it was too European in its outlook and even that it was too French. The impetus was toward a more international organization. Just as

Interpol required a process of "intergovernmentalization" to clarify its legal status, so some sort of internal "internationalization" seemed called for.

In 1967 the Lebanese delegation had moved to create four deputy secretaries general and to arrange for each one to be selected from a different continent. The motion was defeated, but not before the feelings behind it had been vented. A formal resolution was passed to the effect that Interpol should become an "equal opportunity employer" by having persons of more nationalities represented on its staff.

The meeting in Washington seemed to be the beginning of a new era in Interpol history. During the next ten years the General Assembly met five times in non-European capitals, twice in Asia. It seems curious, however, that at a time when crime has been increasing in all parts of the world and when even the smallest states seek admission to Interpol, certain large, powerful nations remain aloof. Since 1969 Fiji, Burundi, Iceland, Lesotho, Nauru, Mali, and Mauritius have joined, but the nations of the Eastern bloc other than Yugoslavia have remained outside.

The reason for the self-exclusion of the Soviet Union, Poland, Czechoslovakia, and the other countries of eastern Europe does not seem to be the absence of criminal activity within their boundaries, for these countries do have crime, of course. The reason seems to be a matter of principle. Interpol insists that crime and politics be kept separate, but an embezzler, for example, in the Soviet Union is accused, tried, and punished as though he had committed an act against the state very much like treason. Eastern bloc police are evidently not expected to differentiate between what Interpol's constitution defines as common law crimes and political crimes. Interpol subscribes to the Universal Declaration of Human Rights, which is a specific countermeasure against the secret and political police traditions of eastern Europe. The nonpolitical administration of criminal justice may fall short of ideal in some countries, but it seems important that a world organization with Interpol's influence should be its advocate within the framework of the larger principles of human rights.

4
Interpol in Action

On September 18, 1965, five people left South America for the United States, three men using the names Geneyro, Poletta, and Ramos, and two women, Maria Ipanien Taschian and Ingeborg Skoruppa. Point of departure for Geneyro and Ramos was Belém, Brazil. Poletta left from Montevideo in Uruguay. The two women began their journey in São Paolo, Brazil.

Flying separate routes, they island-hopped across the Caribbean on Pan American planes. At several stopovers, the men cashed fraudulent cashier's checks and stolen traveler's checks. The five joined up in Miami on the weekend of the twenty-fifth, and the men cashed a few more phony checks.

On the twenty-seventh they started for New York in a rented car. When they reached the city, they turned in the car, rented another, and spent the following ten days passing phony and stolen checks. On the evening of October 11, they turned in the second car, rented a station wagon, and checked out of the Holland Hotel on West Forty-second Street. Canada was to be their destination. The luggage piled in the back of the station wagon held a quarter of a million dollars in uncashed bad and stolen checks. In the lobby of the hotel were two New York City detectives.

At 5 P.M. that day, the phone had rung in the squad room of the Sixteenth Precinct on West Forty-seventh Street. A jewelry shop on Sixth Avenue had been hit with two bad checks within the hour. Two of the squad's detectives drove over in an unmarked squad car. One of the owners of the store, Louis Modell, was out looking for his watchman, who had been sent to follow the check-passers. The detectives drove into the Exchange—the block on Forty-seventh Street between Fifth and Sixth Avenues known as the New York Diamond Exchange—where they found Modell. Modell handed over two fraudulent checks that he had accepted as payment for a diamond ring, described the check-passers, and gave the license number of an automobile his watchman had seen one of them enter. The detectives traced the car to a local Hertz office, where the records showed that the driver had given the Holland Hotel as his address.

At the hotel, the detectives were questioning the desk clerk when he indicated that one of the suspects was standing behind them. The two detectives then watched a man with a Latin appearance pay his hotel bill and then join two other men and two women. With nine suitcases among them, the group left the hotel and loaded the luggage into a station wagon parked in front. The detectives moved in, identified themselves, and asked the five to accompany them to the precinct house.

In the squad room Modell identified one of the men as the check-passer and the other two as his companions. The women were unknown to him and were allowed to leave after questioning. The three men carried passports that identified them as Jorge Washington Gonzales Ramos, Francesco

Poletta, and Raul Domingo Geneyro. Ramos, who, according to Modell, had endorsed the checks and accepted the ring, at first denied everything but finally agreed to return the ring. At that point the whole matter could have been dropped at the discretion of the investigating detectives. The ring had been returned, the check fraud had been thwarted, and no one had been hurt. The police, however, were not satisfied. Ramos had used the name Peter Wichers when offering the phony checks and had shown Modell an Austrian passport in that name to verify his endorsement. At the police station he had identified himself by a Uruguayan passport in the other name.

The three men were asked to open their suitcases. The cases contained hundreds of checks, nineteen passports from seven different countries, a number of rubber stamps of the kind used in various countries to stamp passport visas, bottles of ink and ink pads, ink eradicators, a numbering machine, a magnifying glass, and special pens and other paraphernalia associated with the art of forgery.

The detectives spent the rest of the night telephoning for representatives to come in from the United States Secret Service, the FBI, the Bureau of Customs, the State Department, the Internal Revenue Service, the Immigration and Naturalization Service, the New York City Criminal Investigation Bureau, the Pickpocket and Confidence Squad, the Safe and Loft Squad, and the borough commander's office. The next day they made further calls to executives of various banks around the city and to the consulates of countries whose passports had been found in the luggage.

All through the night and into the next morning, investigators from the various agencies and banks came with interpreters to question the suspects, who told them absolutely nothing. They claimed that this was their first visit to the United States, but they seemed to know the rights of suspects and refused to answer questions. They were held for arraignment, charged with grand larceny and fraud, and fingerprinted. Searches of the files of the New York City Police, the State Police, and the FBI turned up no records concerning any of them.

According to the evidence found in the suitcases, at least seven major banks had been swindled over a period of ten days; yet no one had filed a complaint or reported anything amiss to the police. If Modell had not reported his two bad checks, the check-passers would have disappeared into Canada with their loot and forgery supplies intact.

Obviously this was not a simple local crime. A large-scale crime of international scope was indicated, but it did not seem to come into focus as a court case. A small army of investigators went to work on it. After three weeks of digging, they were unable to say exactly who the suspects were or where they had come from. The federal prosecutor for the Southern District of New York declined to prosecute. The city district attorney agreed to prosecute, but his assistants assigned to the case did not seem to think that there was very much to it. To them it looked like a minor charge of grand larceny or fraud. The accused had entered the country illegally; if they were simply ordered to leave, the taxpayers would be saved the expense of a trial and their imprisonment.

The prosecutor was scheduled to go before the grand jury on November 9. By November 4 the investigators knew no more about Geneyro, Ramos, and Poletta than they had on the day of their arrest. Then, on November 5, a telex message was handed to one of the city detectives. It said that Raul Domingo Geneyro, who claimed to have been born in Uruguay and never to have been arrested, was in reality Emilio Manera, born in Italy, a dangerous criminal who was wanted as a fugitive from justice. It further asked the New York City Police to assist the United States Immigration and Naturalization Service in detaining Manera until extradition proceedings could be arranged.

The message had come from Interpol Rome. On November

8 a second telex message, also from Interpol Rome, gave further details of Manera's criminal record, including a series of convictions from which he was a fugitive. It also identified Ramos as a criminal fugitive named Wissocq-Bo who operated under a number of aliases. The message asked for a set of Poletta's fingerprints and information from the documents found in his possession so that an identification of him could be verified.

According to Interpol, Manera, alias Geneyro, alias a number of other names, was wanted for swindling, drug traffic, receiving stolen property, theft, and forgery in Milan, Bologna, Cortina d'Ampezzo, Bolzano, and Rome. The other two were likewise identified. Interpol had reached across international boundaries. These international criminals were ultimately brought before the bar of justice to answer for their crimes because of information in Interpol's massive files.

By July, 1971, these General Secretariat files contained over 1,562,700 cards bearing the names of individuals listed alphabetically and phonetically, nearly 91,000 fingerprint cards, and almost 7,000 indexed photographs of specialized criminals. The files have increased at the rate of 10 to 12 percent annually. The criminal investigators of all Interpol members have ready access to the intelligence stored in these files.

To pluck from so vast a storehouse of cards, fingerprints, and photos precisely the information needed about a particular criminal is no mean accomplishment. Interpol is asked to do it every day. Persons at Interpol headquarters are trained to pull a dossier in seconds, in minutes if the situation is complicated. Requests to identify suspects and recount their criminal biographies, if any, come to Interpol from around the world.

In retrospect, it seems odd that the New York and United States authorities should have gone more than three weeks without positive identifications of the three suspects in that bank swindling case. Interpol files at the time had extensive and detailed information on them and was equipped to furnish dossiers that would have been immediately informative to the investigators, the prosecutor, and the court. The reason for the lack of communication in this case lies in the unusual relationship that existed between the United States and Interpol, and the details of the relationship are explained in Chapter 6.

The core of the General Secretariat's organization is the International Criminal Police Coordination Division. In addition to the alphabetical and phonetic card files, the division keeps special card indexes for the names of boats, license numbers of suspect cars, the number of passports used by individuals under surveillance, and the other seemingly trivial details that make up the mosaics of criminal intelligence work. Cards are cross-referenced to dossiers.

The name files include the aliases of all criminals who have been brought to Interpol's attention. The phonetic system makes it possible to overcome the vagaries of language and spelling so that detectives as far apart, literally and figuratively, as Australia and Zambia have at their disposal a common system of communication. Through this system, the organization can serve police agencies in Indonesia, Indiana, Israel, Jordan, Japan, or anywhere else. Even Chinese has been accommodated phonetically in this dual phonetic-alphabetical name file—no mean feat. It is a sort of universal key for entering the maze of files and indexes into which Interpol has sorted the world of international crime.

In addition to the relatively small, selective fingerprint file, there are three special filing systems unique to Interpol—the portrait parle, the analytic index, and the punch card index.

The portrait parle, or "talking picture" file, is comprised of photographs of criminals indexed according to a six-point formula, based on bone structure and adapted from the Bertillon system. Each person's face and head are assigned a numerical code that can be filed for fast retrieval. This system helps put the finger on wanted criminals even if they try to alter their photographic appearances by such means as grimacing, stuffing objects into their cheeks and noses, or undergoing plastic surgery. The portrait parle penetrates these subterfuges, reducing the subject of each portrait to a number of codified individual characteristics that cannot be disguised no matter how he puffs out his cheeks or has his face lifted.

The analytic index is an ingenious screening file. Most police files the world over, including new, computerized systems, are based on one characteristic of the subject, such as finger patterns, photographs, names, serial numbers, and so on. The analytic index file is based on a "whole person" approach. It comes into play particularly when an investigator is unable to supply a reliable name, fingerprints, or a photograph for screening a suspect. If, on the other hand, he or his witnesses are highly observant, and he is able to forward to Saint-Cloud information describing the suspect's voice and manner, his walk, his complexion, his estimated dimensions, or other distinguishing features, such an inquiry could be screened through the analytic index.

This file is composed of specially designed cards, each marked by a colored clip-on tab. Each tab refers to one particular physical or behavioral characteristic or mental trait or quirk. The cards are compiled from detailed forms containing information garnered from police reports. When properly filed, a drawer of these cards looks like a miniature colorful forest of upright tabs. Actually, the scatter of their colors is the key to locating wanted criminals.

The forms behind these colored tab cards list 177 separate characteristics such as nationality, place where crime was committed, probable race, apparent height, face, complexion, pigmentation, teeth, voice, gait, general demeanor, traits of character, vices, scars, moles, tattoos, amputations, deformities, habits and peculiarities, and so on. The subheadings under "general demeanor," for instance, include quick-tempered, proud, dignified, subservient, and sexy. Those under "habits and peculiarities" include tic or twitch, nail-biting, throat-clearing, and eye-blinking. Gaits are described as slouchy or stiff, a face may be square, round, long, or droopy.

As the chief of this section explains it, "Starting with only a few characteristics, or even one, it is possible to come up with a name and a dossier. The colored tab cards permit us to narrow the search by features that are likely to be unique to an individual. The assumption is that everyone has something of his own. If a police agency inquires, for example, about a gold smuggler who looks like a Eurasian, is short in stature, walks with toes pointed out, speaks in a high-pitched voice, and has a small mole under his left ear, we have something to work with. We are able to pull index cards with certain colored tabs, put them together, and have them indicate a specific dossier or a couple of possibilities which, with fingerprints and photographs, can be made available to the agency that is pursuing the case."

The third of these original specialized identification systems is the punch card index. Each card refers to one "element" or circumstance in a crime and has enough space for one thousand holes. Each hole indicates a particular dossier. When several "element" cards are placed on top of one another, a pattern emerges that indicates dossiers of possible suspects.

In addition to having two groups that handle files and fingerprint identification, the International Criminal Police Coordinating Division also has five groups to study the results of investigations and to coordinate intelligence work. Each of these groups concentrates on particular categories of crime. Group C works on murder, burglary, assault, larceny, pocket-picking, sleight-of-hand theft, car theft, stolen articles, and missing persons, including juveniles. Group D works on bank fraud, substitution theft, embezzlement, swindling, worthless checks, smuggling, and forgery. Group E concerns itself with drugs, morals offenses, and traffic in women. Group F is concerned with counterfeiting. It publishes *Counterfeits and Forgeries Review*, which catalogs all issues of bogus money known to be in current circulation and is available to police agencies, banks, and certain kinds of financial institutions. Group G covers general economic and financial crimes.

Counterfeits and Forgeries Review is only one of the publications for which the Secretariat is responsible. Other publications give national police officers an international view of the crimes they are concerned with—substitution theft, gold traffic, diamond traffic, drug traffic—and often supply photographs and descriptions of identified international criminals engaged in each kind of crime.

Sometimes police are unable to zero in on an offender and bring him directly to justice; there are times when an offender is on the run, in hiding, or about to make new criminal moves, and is ominously silent. Interpol has devised a method by which concerned law enforcement agencies can track such an individual.

This method involves the "circulation." The circulations come in three colors, green, blue, and red, indicated by a square of color in a corner of the document. A green circulation gives notice of the whereabouts of an individual in whose criminal career a police agency is particularly interested, enabling the agency to pick up his trail or make special arrangements to follow through. A blue circulation is a widespread inquiry for information about an offender from any country that knows about him from past activity or that can locate him and run down new information on actual or potential criminal activity. A red circulation is a request to all nations to seek, find, and detain a criminal wanted by police to answer for specific crimes in a particular country. It also gives due notice that the authorities of that country intend to institute extradition proceedings to get him back.

The circulations, therefore, comprise a mutual aid system. For example, a country that is host to a large international event like a World's Fair or Olympic games is likely to be a magnet for the best pickpockets of all nations. Police of the host country can call on Interpol for a blue circulation asking police of other nations to supply information about professionals who are missing from their usual haunts and requesting intelligence reports on those who are heading for the international event. When a police agency has conducted successful countermeasures against pocket-picking and knows that there is an exodus in progress, it can initiate a green circulation alerting the police of sister nations to the whereabouts of the criminals that are on the move.

Each circulation includes a summary of the individual's criminal career so that police can start with a fair chance of success in dealing with the offender. The World's Fairs in Brussels and Montreal, for instance, are said to have been outstandingly free of pocket-picking because of advance police preparations in which international professional criminals were turned back at the border or nabbed, jailed, and deported before they could start operating.

Circulations have to be prepared carefully, especially red circulations, for reasons of both tactics and international good will. When received, they must be used skillfully. Most countries permit their police to detain a person for a limited period of time; then he must be charged before a magistrate or released. If the evidence is not sufficient to continue to hold him and he is let go, he is alerted to the fact that he is being hunted and can take defensive or evasive action. The circulation must give the cooperating police the information they can work with. At the same time, they must adapt it to the laws or regulations of criminal justice in their own country. To do otherwise would be to risk public criticism that would ultimately reflect on Interpol's effectiveness.

A circulation—in accord with Interpol policy—must genuinely concern a crime against common law and must be free of political overtones or personal harassment. Before a red circulation can be issued, Interpol must be assured that substantial evidence exists and that three specific conditions have been met: the offense is a crime against common law; a warrant or order for arrest has been issued; and the nation

requesting arrest will start extradition proceedings as soon as
it is notified that the wanted man has been detained.

The problem of extradition is one that has engaged Interpol's attention almost from the moment of its inception, for
it is a perplexing and sometimes frustrating problem of vital
importance to an organization that deals with crime on an international level.

Of what value are highly skilled police work and scientific
detection when the criminal can evade his pursuers by keeping
out of their territorial jurisdiction? Honest citizens become
skeptical of criminal justice under such circumstances, and
diligent law-enforcement officers' frustrations can drive them
to cynicism.

In the case of Manera, for example, it was obvious to the
two New York detectives from the first that he was an experienced major criminal, but under the vagaries of the New York
system of criminal justice—the only lawful authority under
which Manera was originally being held—the offense for
which he had been arrested was regarded as minor, and he
stood ready to walk out of custody. Guided by his lawyer,
Manera agreed to plead guilty to grand larceny and received a
suspended sentence. The judge also ordered him to leave the
country at once. That order suited Manera since he was a
wanted man in Italy, and Italian authorities now knew where
to find him. At one point he let it be known that he had been a
victim of Mussolini's political repression and had fled to South
America, where he had taken on Uruguayan citizenship.
Through his interpreters, Manera claimed that this meant he
should be protected against Italian efforts to take him and that
he should, in accordance with American law, be permitted to
go to a South American country of his own choosing—
Uruguay.

So with his suspended sentence and his court order to leave
the United States, Manera was ready to be freed, but the Interpol bulletins changed all that. The red circulation wanted
notice traced his criminal history back to 1950, enumerated

his convictions by various courts, and summarized his involvement with an international gang of criminals who specialized in swindling by forging bank transfer orders and cashing stolen traveler's checks. It also reported that he was wanted by the courts of West Germany for forgery and receiving stolen property. The Interpol circulation was the means by which Manera was kept out of circulation. He was reindicted by federal officers, taken into their custody, and prosecuted for federal crimes in a federal court. Meanwhile, Italian authorities had more time to work on their side of the problem.

In its original telex, Interpol Rome had declared that Italy intended to move for Manera's extradition. The extradition treaty between the United States and Italy, however, calls for a highly complicated procedure that involves the State Department, the courts, legal counsel hired by the Italian government, and a great deal of time.

Both United States and Italian law-enforcement officials knew that the one simple way to handle the case was through deportation. Manera's lawyers did their best to get him deported to a succession of Latin American countries, only to have each country reject the request. Finally the only deportation channel that remained open led back to Italy. Interpol Rome, through the national central bureau of each South American country, had let it be known that it had a wanted notice out on Manera. When Manera did finally return to Italy to serve his time, it was not through extradition but through deportation.

The complexities of extradition are many. No country has an obligation to surrender a fugitive from justice to any other country unless it has "contracted" to do so in an extradition treaty. Yet even when such a treaty exists, many crimes may not be covered. For example, so-called fiscal offenses are traditionally excluded, as are political, military, or religious offenses. Large numbers of draft resisters from the United States bear witness to this as they continue to avoid U.S. draft laws by living in Canada, Sweden, Denmark, and other countries.

The rule of thumb governing extradition treaties seems to be that the offenses specified must involve double criminality; that is, they must be recognized as crimes by *both* parties to the treaty. Federal crimes rarely fall into this category, except, mainly, narcotics smuggling, counterfeiting, and forgery offenses. Tax offenses usually are not extraditable crimes; nor, with few exceptions, are crimes of smuggling or those involving securities and exchange violations. In some countries mail fraud is not a crime.

The following crimes, because they are recognized as crimes by other countries, are covered by almost all United States treaties of extradition: murder; rape; bigamy (though not in Chile, Bolivia, Denmark, and Panama); arson; certain crimes at sea, including robbery, sinking or destroying vessels, mutiny, and assault with intent to do bodily harm; robbery; burglary; forgery; counterfeiting; embezzlement; larceny; fraud; perjury; and kidnapping.

The reason for what may appear to be lack of cooperation has little to do with crime, but rather has a great deal to do with traditions of national sovereignty. Traditionally, one sovereign state does not take lightly the act of surrendering a person to another. But in recent times, in response to ideas pressed by Interpol, many nations have changed laws and practices to reduce criminals' immunity.

In effect, each case of extradition under the terms of an extradition treaty becomes not only a legal problem but a diplomatic one as well. A request for extradition must be transmitted from one country to another through regular diplomatic channels; once it has been received and acceded to, then and then only are the police able to go into the courts for the extradition order. And that may not be the end of the matter, since the court has to rule on each case, and there may be appeals to higher courts, and so on. Meanwhile, unless the accused has committed an offense against the laws of the country he is in, he is free to come and go, and that, for an experienced criminal, means opportunity to escape.

Interpol has attempted to mitigate the extradition problem by encouraging its member countries to write more and better extradition treaties, by supporting international conferences and conventions concerning extradition, and, most important, by developing the concept of provisional arrest. Provisional arrest means that on the basis of a properly arranged police request from one country, the police of another country will take custody of an accused or convicted offender and hold him or her for a limited period of time while the requesting country processes an extradition.

Three requirements must be met for the police of the second country to comply with such a request. A red circulation from Interpol must be issued on the criminal; this must be followed by a telegraphic or written request from the secretary general of Interpol as soon as the offender is located; and the secretary general's request must be followed up with a similar request from the national central bureau of the country involved. In other words, the wanted notice must be followed immediately by a confirmation that the requesting country is proceeding at once to exercise its extradition rights through diplomatic channels, and affirmation must be in hand of the fact that the wanted person is accused of a common law crime.

While the criminal is being provisionally held, the country that wants him takes appropriate action for extradition— usually supplying the necessary documents and its own domestic court orders, then hiring a law firm in the holding country to represent the other country in court so that a court order allowing the extradition can be obtained. In each country that observes this procedure, there must be a specific, lawful authority under which the police have the power to make such arrests. During the period of June 1, 1970, to June

1, 1971, 554 individuals were arrested as a result of wanted notices published by the Interpol General Secretariat or other intervention.

Most Western nations have adopted some form of provisional arrest. The United States, however, had not done so as of the start of the 1970s and was retaining a strictly interpreted extradition procedure.

Obviously, Interpol must be sensitive to many diplomatic, political, and legal factors in using its vast resources and carrying out its functions. Cooperation among member countries, resulting in effective arrangements to detain international criminals without threatening the sovereignty of any national government, are very often dependent on mutual confidence, respect, good will, and understanding—those intangibles of human relations.

5
The Interpol
Organization

INTERPOL is usually described as a unique organization. In addition to the functions embodied in its national police agencies, its private radio network, its telex network, and its system for gathering, exchanging, storing, and retrieving intelligence on criminal activities, Interpol is a deliberative body at whose meetings problems and viewpoints of diverse nations and cultures are examined, debated, and, when necessary, reconciled. The attempts to attain the members' common goal of suppressing crime sometimes entail economic or social dislocations for one or several member nations in order that all may benefit. This proved to be the case when Interpol faced the problem of drug traffic. Sometimes a problem must be worked out on a technical level before it can be presented on the governmental level, where emotions, national pride, or political considerations may complicate the possibilities for agreement on a plan of action, as with the problem of skyjacking.

61

Such problems are considered and solutions found in Interpol's General Assembly. There, East and West, Arab and Israeli, Christian and Buddhist, and persons of all national and racial variations meet and share experiences and concerns. The assembly is the heart and head of the crime-fighting organism; it is also Interpol's governing authority. Each member, an official police agency designated by the government of its country, may appoint one or more delegates to the General Assembly, one of whom is designated to be the head of the delegation by his government's authority. Specialists in subjects on a particular agenda may be included in the delegation.

In accord with the general regulations set forth in the constitution, the General Assembly meets in ordinary session at least once a year and in extraordinary session whenever the executive committee or a majority of the membership so requests. Each annual session is held in a different country, usually—though not always—in the capital city. Extraordinary sessions are always held at Interpol headquarters in Saint-Cloud.

The General Assembly is described in official Interpol literature as sovereign in all matters affecting the organization. It decides general policy, establishes the methods and norms of cooperation among members, adopts the work program presented by the secretary general, approves the budget, elects the executive committee and the officers, and adopts resolutions and recommendations on matters of international police cooperation. A recent General Assembly session in Ottawa in September, 1971, drew 287 delegates representing 92 of the 111 countries that were members at the time.

The executive committee is composed of the president, three vice-presidents, nine delegates, and two auditors. Each of these fifteen members is from a different country, and geographical distribution is considered in their selection. The president is elected for a four-year term, each of the vice-presidents for three years, and the nine delegates for three years each. Only the president can be reelected immediately upon completing a term in office, thus ensuring a steady turn-over of the committee membership. The executive committee meets twice a year. Their duties include the supervision of the execution of assembly decisions, the preparation of the as-sembly's agendas, and the supervision of the administration and work of the secretary general. The committee may also submit projects and programs to the assembly. The president chairs all General Assembly sessions and executive committee meetings, ensures that the organization acts according to the decisions made by its governing bodies, and maintains con-stant contact with the secretary general.

Like the secretary general of the United Nations, the secre-tary general of Interpol bears the ultimate responsibility for the organization's vital functions. He is appointed on the rec-ommendation of the executive committee and with the ap-proval of the General Assembly for a period of five years. He may succeed himself as often as the committee chooses to rec-ommend him and the assembly approves, but he must retire from office at the age of sixty-five. He directs the organiza-tion's operations at headquarters and plays an active role in the work of each General Assembly. He is the senior perma-nent full-time official of Interpol, and as such he hires the staff and supervises its work, administers the budget, and organizes and directs the organization's permanent departments ac-cording to the instructions of the assembly and the executive committee, the two bodies to whom he must answer. He also submits proposals for programs and projects to the assembly and the executive committee. Like the other officers of In-terpol, the secretary general represents the organization in the exercise of his duties and not any particular country; neither he nor any member of his staff may ask for or accept instruc-tions from any government or any authority outside of In-terpol.

The present secretary general is Jean Nepote. Nepote was born in Bolbec in the French province of Normandy in 1915.

He holds a degree in law from the University of Lyon and entered government service in 1935 at the prefecture of the Rhône Department in Lyon. In 1941 he was appointed to the French police force as a commissaire and went to the general headquarters of the Sûreté Nationale.

When the ICPC was reestablished in 1946, he was assigned to become assistant to the new secretary general, Louis Ducloux. In this position he supervised the operations of various General Secretariat departments, directed the implementation of the organization's principal projects, and often represented Interpol at international meetings. From time to time, he has been asked to participate as an expert in United Nations deliberations.

In 1958 the General Assembly named him deputy secretary general; in 1963, at its annual meeting in Helsinki, it elected him secretary general, and it reelected him in 1968. In 1966 he was promoted by the Sûreté Nationale to the rank of *contrôleur général*. He is a *Chevalier* of the Légion d'Honneur and an *officier* of the Ordre National du Mérite.

At present he is past his middle fifties, a dynamic man who talks quietly, smiles readily, and answers questions with precision. A man of average height and size, he usually wears a dark suit and in other surroundings could be taken for a prosperous business executive. At first meeting he may seem reserved, but as he warms up to his favorite subject, Interpol, the reserve diminishes. His eyes give one the impression of alertness and a constant habit of probing. He has long been accustomed to having people who meet him for the first time tell him that they regard his job as a paradox. He heads an organization engaged in a world-wide battle against crime, yet neither he nor any member of his organization is permitted to fire a gun or make an arrest.

His office is on the top floor of the headquarters building in Saint-Cloud. The walls are hung with memorabilia and artifacts that reflect his travels and his world-wide contacts.

When the telephone on his desk interrupts a conversation in his office, he answers quietly, then speaks into the receiver with a Frenchman's animation. As the visitor waits for the telephone conversation to end, his thoughts wander perhaps to the supersleuth so popular in modern crime fiction—suave, glib, and ready at a moment's notice to do battle with the master criminal, employing his cunning, his deadly accurate pistol-shooting, and his lethal fists to bring the criminal to inevitable justice.

Nepote hangs up and turns back to the visitor. For a moment it is a little difficult to turn from the supersleuth of the imagination to this man in a business suit who picks up the conversation where he left off, talking thoughtfully about trends in the social development of nations and the human condition. This is no fighter of gun battles, no intrepid veteran of high-powered auto pursuits, knife-like interrogations, and dramatic arrests. Instead, he exercises a unique power, moving bits of information from here to there, sometimes with startling results.

"I am no 'Monsieur Duval,' " he says, referring to the "Interpol" character in a television series some years back. "Nor am I the employer of a James Bond. You may recall Duval. He traveled from country to country solving the most dangerous and difficult cases, leaving a dozen or so bodies in his wake—completely indifferent to the feelings of his local colleagues."

Nepote smiles as he pauses to consider the mythical Interpol. "The real Interpol," he continues, "is simply a machine for permanent and organized cooperation between the police forces of more than one hundred nations."

When he started with Interpol, its facilities consisted of a typewriter and a duplicating machine, both of which had been through the war, and a tiny office in Paris, courtesy of the French police. From there it was moved to a town house that had formerly been the home of a family called Menier who were descendants of Guy de Maupassant. The organization then moved to the district of Porte Maillot, where it set up its headquarters in the old Luna Park, an administrative site under the control of the ministry of interior. Marcel Sicot, the former secretary general, says in *A la barre de l'Interpol* that the ministry was suffocating for lack of space on this site, necessitating the removal of ICPC's headquarters to available space at 60 Boulevard Gouvion Saint-Cyr, next to the headquarters of the Civil Protection and Fire Department Services.

Despite its limited facilities, the Secretariat seems to have functioned in so remarkable a fashion that by 1950 there were thirty-five countries affiliated with the ICPC. In December, 1955, another transfer took place, this time to a building that had previously housed the Irish Embassy, an originally distinguished town house located not far from l'Etoile. These larger quarters were much in keeping with ICPC's progress in the world. The building had a private courtyard, and its interior had magnificent crystal chandeliers. A curving staircase in the grand style led up from the entrance foyer—appropriate for an international embassy.

It was during this period that the organization changed its name to Interpol. After ten more years, the organization moved into its present permanent headquarters on the Rue Armengaud. The site was purchased in August, 1962—3,325 square meters, about an acre and a quarter, that had once belonged to René Caudron, a pioneer of French aviation. The money for the land purchase came out of the organization's safety and reserve fund, and the building was financed by money from several sources. Among them were the French government, which loaned 3,575,000 Swiss francs; several member nations, which contributed 200,000 Swiss francs; and Interpol's ordinary budget, which contributed 1,347,278 Swiss francs. The French government also refunded taxes paid by firms involved in the building, providing 528,000 Swiss francs. Building, land, and equipment costs totaled some 7 million French francs.

The eight-story building is a long, stylish structure composed of horizontal and vertical design elements in stone, glass, and steel. Its 60,000 square feet of floor space are divided between two separate sections linked by a patio. The seven-story main section houses the General Secretariat offices, radio station, laboratories, a restaurant, and caretakers' flats. The other section houses mainly a conference hall equipped for simultaneous translation into four languages. The building has its own 160-kilowatt generator to provide power in case of a public power failure and a system of pneumatic tubes by which documents are conveyed from department to department.

On May 26, 1967, the new building was officially inaugurated with due ceremony. Present were Christian Fouchet, the French minister of the interior; the members of the diplomatic corps, including forty-two ambassadors and twenty-six representatives of member countries; delegates from the United Nations and the Council of Europe; high-ranking police officers from twenty countries; senior officials from many French government departments; and most of the top French police and *gendarmerie* officials. Among the facilities that the guests inspected were index systems for fast retrieval of data in dossiers, room for more than three million files, the latest photographic equipment in the photo labs, and a number of auditoriums for the seminars and international meetings that Interpol holds regularly.

The articles of the constitution that establish the Secretariat describe it as "an international center in the fight against crime." It is the Secretariat that staffs Interpol's technical and information services and maintains contact with national and international authorities and with the national central bureaus.

It also produces Interpol's publications; organizes and performs the Secretariat's work at all sessions of the General Assembly, the executive committee, and any other body or committee of the organization; and drafts proposals for programs that are presented each year to the assembly and executive committee for approval.

Staffing the headquarters are about 110 people, about 45 of whom are police officers "seconded" from the prefecture of Paris police or the Sûreté. There are also contract employees, civil servants, and police officers on assignment from England, Germany, Sweden, Italy, Canada, and several other countries.

One of the Secretariat's key jobs is establishing and maintaining communications with the national central bureaus. To do this, it operates an international radio network using a dozen remote-controlled transmitters operating on 1–4 kilowatts on decametric waves, powerful enough for communication around the globe. By 1972 thirty-five member countries were in the network. This network, officially known as the International Criminal Police Radio Network, is a "CW" type (Morse Code).

Each station in the network is classified as either a central or a national station. The national stations are grouped into regional networks, and each regional network is linked to the central station. In addition to serving as the hub of its regional network, each central station is linked to the other central stations and routes message traffic for the national central bureaus of its region to those of other regions. The regional central stations are also linked to the headquarters central station in Saint-Cloud. Each regional network serves a major geographic zone. Each national station is expected to maintain continuous contact with the central station of its network. The central stations have established bilateral connections among themselves according to established schedules of frequencies and times of transmission.

The entire network is divided into three main zones. The

Europe-Mediterranean zone includes twenty-three stations: Paris, Belgrade, Copenhagen, Jerusalem, London, Madrid, Oslo, Rabat, Vienna, Algiers, Ankara, Beirut, Brussels, Helsinki, Lisbon, Luxembourg, Rome, Stockholm, Tehran, Tunis, Utrecht, Wiesbaden, and Zürich; the South American zone includes Buenos Aires, Brasília, Caracas, La Paz, Lima, Montevideo, and Santiago; the Southeast Asia zone includes Tokyo, Manila, and Seoul. In addition, three national stations are directly linked to the Saint-Cloud central station: Ottawa, Monrovia, and Washington.

The Interpol communications network includes a telex system as well for the instant relay of hard copy messages. Plans are under way to set up a phototelegraphy network and a system of facsimile transmission that uses ordinary telephone lines.

The General Secretariat is divided into four main divisions and seven specialized groups. Division I, General Administration, attends to the bookkeeping chores and budgets, personnel, equipment, and general correspondence. It compiles the organization's statistics, makes preparations for meetings of the General Assembly, manages such services as the radio network, translations, photography, and press and public relations, and supervises the allotment of funds for technical cooperation.

Division II, International Criminal Police Coordination, handles special aspects of international crimes either on its own initiative or at the request of the police of member countries. In practice it does not investigate crimes, but it does handle special aspects of criminal investigations, follow special cases, study the results of police investigations of selected cases, and coordinate international police efforts. As one of the most vital and complicated of Interpol's functions, this division is broken down into seven operating groups that are responsible for files; fingerprint identification; murder and theft; bank fraud; drugs, morals offenses and traffic in women; counterfeiting and publication of *Counterfeits and Forgeries Review*; economic and financial crimes.

Division III, Research, is the General Secretariat's information and research center for legal and technical questions. One of the principal duties of this division is to keep up with the latest trends in criminology, crime prevention, and the treatment of juveniles. Its staff researches the latest methods of police work and the organization and equipment of police departments all over the world. The staff is in touch with international organizations, criminological associations, penal law societies, and other concerned groups and conferences. They look over more than 250 specialized and professional journals as well as books published in the field in all languages and maintain a ready reference catalog of material from these sources. Members are informed of the materials available through the book review section of the *International Criminal Police Review* and the *Quarterly List of Selected Articles*, a multilingual list of articles from professional journals identified by title, a short summary, and a reference. The *Quarterly List* is sent regularly and without charge to subscribers of the *Review*, and microfilm copies of articles are available to them on request.

An important responsibility of the Research Division is to prepare summaries of data supplied by the national central bureaus and present reports to the General Assembly and other major international organizations and scientific bodies. It is also equipped to describe and elaborate on Interpol policy, and it sometimes makes suggestions concerning the positions police authorities should adopt on police ethics and professional rights. It organizes international seminars that offer advanced professional training to the police officers who attend. It also publishes once every two years an *International Crime Statistics Report*, which contains analyses of crime developments in countries affiliated with Interpol.

The *International Criminal Police Review*, Interpol's

primary publication, is a confidential monthly prepared by the Secretariat's Division IV. Its contributors include specialists on subjects of interest to police forces everywhere, and it reports on new criminal investigation techniques, law and criminology, psychology, forensic medicine, and the entire range of pertinent research. The Secretariat publishes in French and English, and the national central bureau in Madrid translates and prints a Spanish language edition.

The General Secretariat runs up some statistics of its own. For instance, from June 1, 1970, to June 1, 1971, the Secretariat handled 10,875 cases, including 87 cases concerning violence against persons, 472 cases of theft, 145 cases involving motor vehicles, 1,603 cases of fraud, 3,178 counterfeit and forgery cases, 4,660 cases having to do with narcotics, 126 sex and morals offenses, 377 identifications, and 227 miscellaneous cases. It issued international notices for 451 persons and 77 notices about stolen property. As a result of Interpol wanted notices, 554 individuals were arrested. Interpol also identified 88 individuals and supplied 8,964 items of information to national central bureaus.

By comparison, during the reporting period of June 1, 1966, to June 1, 1967, the Secretariat handled a total of 4,124 cases, an increase of 198 cases from the previous reporting period of 1965–66, but a far cry from the 5,045 by which its case load increased between June, 1967, and June, 1970. (All this with a staff of just over 100 persons.) From 1967 to 1970, the number of counterfeit and forgery cases more than doubled while the number of narcotics cases more than tripled.

The upward trends of these figures are not intended to reflect the status of international crime; rather, they indicate the growing rate of Interpol's involvement in casework as distinct from general services, research, and policy debate. In each case, the Secretariat was called on for assistance by the police force of a member nation in the investigation, identification, or arrest of an offender.

In 1969–70, the Secretariat improved the efficiency of its records on highly specialized criminals by reorganizing its classification methods. New specialized files were set up to hold the information kept by the specialized groups that deal with specific types of offenses. Retrieval of information from these files can be based on a variety of criteria, including the age of the offender or selected physical characteristics. The Secretariat's programs of recent years have included detailed reports on counterfeiting and drug trafficking, a twenty-five-page bibliography of works on firearms identification, a list of seamen drug smugglers, and the development of a typewriter identification system. By 1970 *Counterfeits and Forgeries Review* had attained more than 5,700 subscribers and more than 2,000 subscribers to a German regional edition. During a single year, the *Review* had described 105 new counterfeit types and 173 new genuine notes and coins. Its staff counterfeit specialists had analyzed 456 counterfeits, and the specifications of 83 genuine notes were registered and filed.

The scope of the work of the General Secretariat is indicated in the variety of reports originating from its program of activities—the use of computers in police work, developments in juvenile delinquency, the use of drugs among young people, traffic in obscene publications, the detection of anonymous telephone calls, and a project to set up an African Higher Police Academy.

In addition to preparing its own reports, the staff of Interpol assists others in research. In the year ending June 30, 1970, the Secretariat supplied 69 research or bibliographical studies at the request of police services and research workers in 25 countries; it supplied 33 police services and research workers in 15 countries with microfilms of 494 articles or reports.

Most of the Secretariat's work is coordinated with that of the national central bureaus. In countries with a national or federal police organization, the NCB is usually established at its headquarters. In other countries the government has to designate which agency has the responsibility.

Though the national central bureaus are today authorized by Interpol's constitution, they were originally established as an afterthought following the organization of the International Criminal Police Commission in 1923. Two years after ICPC began to function, an international congress on penitentiaries was held in London. On the agenda appeared the question, "How can the fight against international criminals be made more efficient from country to country?" During discussion, Belgian and English delegates recommended that each country set up a central police authority whose job it would be to communicate directly with similar authorities in other countries. The English delegate, Sir Basil Thompson, suggested that ideally this role should be undertaken by a branch of the police in each national capital. These suggestions became part of a draft international convention that was presented in 1926 to a joint meeting of an International Police Congress and the ICPC's third annual assembly in Berlin by Alfred Keffer, chief of the Brussels police.

The following year, the annual assembly of ICPC adopted a resolution that read: "The Commission expresses the wish that its members suggest to their countries, if such a service does not already exist, the setting up of a bureau of national and international criminal records for the rapid exchange of information on international criminals with the bureaus of other countries."

The resolution brought positive results almost immediately. During 1927 and 1928, central bureaus were set up in Vienna, Berlin, Amsterdam, Brussels, Paris, and a number of other capitals. The telling is far more simple than the actual doing, for at the time most police forces were decentralized to a greater extent than they are today, and the problems involved in setting up such bureaus were far more complex.

In 1946, when the ICPC was revived, Florent Louwage, then president of the organization, mentioned the national central bureaus in his opening speech to the General Assembly, but no mention of them was made in the constitution. The General Secretariat drew the attention of the membership to the importance of the roles the national central bureaus had come to play in the organization's operation in an article in the *International Criminal Police Review*. Then, in 1947, two reports on the bureaus were presented to the General Assembly at its sixteenth session. The assembly responded by adopting a resolution to recognize the national bureaus as "the fundamental pillars of the international cooperation restored by the ICPC." The resolution also stipulated that the bureaus would centralize and coordinate all documentation having to do with national and international criminals and would act as liaisons in criminal matters between foreign police departments and with the international office of the ICPC in Paris. Subsequent resolutions at succeeding assembly sessions continued to reaffirm the duties and importance of the national central bureaus until finally, in 1956, the new constitution established them as integral parts of the Interpol structure.

A report on national central bureau policy submitted by Secretary General Nepote to the thirty-fourth session of the General Assembly in Rio de Janeiro in 1965 defines a national central bureau as "the body which in each country has been appointed to be the foothold in that country for international police cooperation within the framework of the I.C.P.C.-INTERPOL . . . at national level the correspondent, the representative, the competent responsible authority of the Organization; consequently . . . the national center for matters of police cooperation. Its role is primary."

All the reasons cited in 1927 in favor of the establishment

of national central bureaus still hold today, even more strongly than they did then.

Police forces vary from country to country both in number and in the complexity of their structures; therefore, in countries that have more than one police force, problems of jurisdiction having to do with international crime are solved by the presence of a national bureau.

Such a bureau takes care to insure efficient international cooperation, for that is its principal function. Difficulties that are bound to arise because of language differences are more easily ironed out by a bureau that has the necessary specialists on its staff. It is essential to have delicate relations handled by an agency specifically attuned to the nuances and subtleties that accompany such an international effort.

The establishment of national central bureaus also facilitates the achievement of Interpol's goals by centralizing information concerning the activities of criminals and passing it through recognized channels. This requires the use of highly complex and powerful facilities, particularly communications facilities, which are best operated as part of a service that has wide jurisdiction.

Police cooperation within the framework of Interpol often calls for the mobilization of large resources for the pursuit and capture of a criminal and for the legal proceedings that follow. A strong police department with adequate jurisdictional authority is required in each country as its NCB.

Setting up the network of national central bureaus proved to be less difficult than might have been expected because of the ICPC bureaus already in existence. Most countries had no trouble designating the police unit to fulfill the role since a particularly well-placed unit within the existing police organization was usually able to take on the job almost immediately. These were usually high-level departments whose heads automatically became the heads of the Interpol bureaus. As time went on, the fundamental aims of the bureaus expanded beyond acting as central information exchange agencies, initiating international investigations, and transmitting requests and identifications. The bureaus now take part in technical and theoretical studies and act as channels for information and officer training in cooperation with police forces and law courts in the countries in which they operate. Each bureau chief is usually a member of his country's delegation at Interpol's General Assembly meetings.

In broad terms, national central bureaus are the points of contact among member countries for the coordination and liaison of international criminal investigative requirements in all forms. They serve as points of contact for local police branches or forces in states, provinces, and towns, customs and immigration offices, and other federal agencies such as treasury departments, narcotics bureaus, and so on. They are often the operative units of liaison for several international agreements, including the European Convention on Extradition and the European Convention on Mutual Assistance in Criminal Matters.

The goals of national central bureau relationships are speed and efficiency through directness and informality. Each bureau maintains constant liaison with the General Secretariat in Saint-Cloud.

Since national central bureaus are directed and staffed by experienced police officers, the question arises whether or not a bureau itself ever takes direct police action. Interpol policy specifies that in normal situations the national central bureau should refrain from action while the national police carry out the actual investigation, arrest, and related activities. It is conceivable, however, that, in exceptional circumstances and given the approval of the police force involved, an NCB could take charge of a particular case. Such a situation would be a rarity, however. Interpol personnel engage almost entirely in intelligence and liaison functions.

An example of the long-established national central

bureaus is Italy's Interpol unit. The Italians have participated in Interpol since its founding in 1923. The chief is a career police official in the Administration of Public Security of Italy's Ministry of Interior. Like the chiefs of other bureaus, he goes once a year with several colleagues to meet face to face with the men at the other ends of the bureau's telephone, telex, and cable lines at the annual General Assembly session. There, he and his men spend a week renewing old acquaintances and making new ones and discussing problems, obstacles, and proposals relating to the systematic business of controlling criminals and criminality. At these encounters each man takes the measure of his counterparts in other lands, testing and judging their professionalism to his own satisfaction.

Backed by a small staff of professional police officers, the chief of the Italian bureau is responsible for all criminal police investigations conducted outside Italy at the request of his country's courts, ordinary police, *carabinieri*, and customs officials. At the same time he handles all requests from foreign police agencies for investigations within Italy of criminal matters of concern to them.

All members of Interpol have access to Italy's aid in criminal investigations, and Italy expects reciprocal aid from each of them. Recently a gruesome sex murder occurred in a small mountain town in central Italy. Painstaking investigation resulted in the identification of a suspect who could not be located. Because he had served in the military forces in North Africa, a wanted notice was circulated to the police in North African countries through the NCB in Rome. The case lay dormant for a year; then police in Ethiopia arrested a European on a charge of attempted robbery. The suspect claimed that he was a Greek merchant seaman and showed ID papers for substantiation. While making a routine check of their files of international notices, however, the Ethiopian police found a set of fingerprints on a wanted notice from Italy that matched those of their suspect. A telex message to Interpol Rome was channeled to the investigators in the mountain town. They had kept the case open, and this news spurred them back into action. The revived investigation established the man's identity, and he was returned to Italy to stand trial.

Despite its name, Interpol Rome is not actually situated in Rome itself but rather in the EUR suburb of Rome. It is housed in a rectangular marble building, part of an elegantly designed complex of government buildings of the Administration of Public Security of the Ministry of Interior. The chief's office is on the fifth floor, adjacent to a suite occupied by his staff. Its furnishings include a large sofa and deep, upholstered armchairs grouped around a hospitable coffee table. Elsewhere in the building is a room filled with cabinets stuffed with files.

Contrast Interpol Rome headquarters with those of the central bureaus in other countries. In Paris, the French NCB is housed in a gloomy turn-of-the-century building not far from the Place de la Concorde. It occupies several drab, cramped offices on the fifth floor of Number 11 Rue des Saussaies, where the superintendent in charge wedges himself behind a desk immediately adjacent to a group of filing cabinets, a couple of chairs, and an accumulation of folders, files, and reports. Despite these unprepossessing quarters, the caliber of police work is highly regarded, and the head of France's national central bureau is usually one of the country's top-ranking police officials. Customarily he is also director of the Central de la Police Judiciare Nationale, which is responsible for all criminal investigations throughout France. Besides the superintendent, Interpol Paris has a staff of about fifteen, which includes *officiers de police* (detective inspectors), *officiers de police adjoints* (detective sergeants), and an administrative staff.

In Wiesbaden, the West German bureau is housed in a huge, modern complex of airy white structures two, three, and five stories high in a quiet suburban setting. In the United States, Interpol Washington is located in the heart of the downtown area, where it occupies a small suite of out-of-the-way offices in the main building of the Department of the Treasury. Despite the wide differences in their quarters, all the national central bureaus around the world have several things in common—a pipeline to one another's criminal records and the means to exchange information quickly on active criminals, to detain them, and to return them to the place where they can be tried and judged for their crimes.

The caseload has increased for the national central bureaus as it has for the Secretariat. During 1966, 31 national central bureaus took part in 838 arrests at the request of other countries, obtained 880 arrests through foreign bureaus, sent 59,454 items of information out to other bureaus, and received 54,567 items from other bureaus. In 1970, with only 17 bureaus reporting, NCB's made 1,065 arrests at the request of other countries, obtained 1,132 arrests through foreign bureaus, sent 108,499 items of information to other NCB's, and received 83,341 items of information from other bureaus.

Like any other international organization, Interpol finances its numerous activities through regular contributions from its members. Each member is classified in one of eleven groups and is expected to pay a number of units into the general budget according to its ability to pay, ranging from sixty units for those in Group 1 to one unit for those in Group 11. The value of each unit is 4,850 Swiss francs, or about $1,262 in U.S. dollars. In practice, each affiliated country makes provisions for its Interpol contribution in its national budget. The money is paid into an Interpol account in the Crédit Lyonnais in Geneva.

Interpol's budget is divided into a number of funds, including a general fund, a reserve fund, and a safety and reserve fund. The last fund provided the money that paid for the land on which the headquarters building stands. Up to 75 percent of the organization's funds may be placed in either long- or short-term investments at the discretion of the secretary general and with the approval of the executive committee. In accord with the articles of the constitution governing its finances, Interpol investments are made with a greater concern for security than for a high rate of interest.

6
The United States
and Interpol

THE case of the five check-passers from South
America that opened Chapter 4, dramatically illustrates a lesson that still had to be learned by American law-enforcement
officers. After more than three weeks of investigation of the
case by New York police and federal agents, the suspects
remained totally unknown. The two women were released the
first night, and the three men hired lawyers who promptly
asked the courts to release the suspects on the promise that
they leave the country at once and not return.

Instead of being allowed to leave the country, the three
were prosecuted—but only after Interpol had alerted American officials to the fact that the suspects were members of a
vast international criminal conspiracy that had for years been
milking banks in South and North America and Europe. Extensive information on each of the men was on tap at Interpol
headquarters and in the Interpol bureaus of Rome, Paris,
Zürich, Brussels, Wiesbaden, Buenos Aires, Montevideo,

Brasília, and other cities. A simple inquiry cabled or telephoned to any one of these bureaus could have broken the case in forty-eight hours.

The case remained a mystery because the New York police and the federal agents did not ask Interpol; most of them did not know about it. If they had ever heard of Interpol at the time, they probably thought of it in relation to the television program purporting to be about the organization. Luckily, the Interpol bureau in Rome learned of the case through one of its channels and sent cables to the New York police that ended the crooks' anonymity. We shall see in a subsequent chapter that they were indicted, sentenced to prison, fined, and deported to countries from which they had fled as fugitives from justice.

In retrospect it seems incredible that American police officers should have been unaware of the facilities of Interpol and that this state of ignorance should have continued into the 1960s. The explanation is in the on-again, off-again affair that the United States conducted with Interpol for over thirty years. Traditionally, the police in the United States have followed narrow jurisdictional concepts, and their contacts with police in foreign countries have, with few exceptions, been almost nonexistent.

According to Marcel Sicot, former secretary general of Interpol, the Second International Criminal Police Congress in Vienna in 1923 had been attended by Richard Enright, police commissioner of New York City. In 1925 Dr. Johann Schober, chief of the Vienna police and the first president of the ICPC, had been invited by Enright to attend a conference of the International Association of Chiefs of Police in New York. And in 1937 Special Agent Charles A. Appel, Jr., of the Federal Bureau of Investigation had traveled through Europe to observe the latest methods of scientific crime detection that were being used by European police. When he returned to Washington, D.C., he used the information to found the FBI's scientific laboratories.

Aside from individual contacts between United States law enforcement agents and their European counterparts on particular cases, there was very little precedent for foreign collaboration. Then in 1938 the United States joined the ICPC, but that was the year its headquarters in Vienna was taken over by the Nazis. The dismemberment of the organization itself with the outbreak of World War II came the following year. When the war was over and efforts to revive Interpol began, the United States took part. A law passed by Congress in 1938 was still on the books when Interpol was being reactivated in 1946. This law delegated participation to the attorney general of the United States, and he designated the director of the Federal Bureau of Investigation as the representative to the organization.

According to Tom Tullet, a British crime reporter, J. Edgar Hoover was an enthusiastic delegate for several years, but his enthusiasm cooled considerably when Czechoslovakia demanded through Interpol the return of ten refugees who had fled to West Germany. Hoover, said Tullet, felt this was improper under the organization's principles, that it violated the prohibition against involvement in political matters. Hoover withdrew in 1950. The official reason was that the FBI received little benefit from Interpol "due to the nature of its investigative jurisdiction." At least one former FBI agent upholds Tullet's theory, but other sources have suggested other reasons. In Europe it was said that European members were uncomfortable about the FBI's involvement at that time in antisubversive work, which they felt was political.

Whatever the reason, the FBI was out and so was the United States—though not entirely. Various government agents had established informal contacts and relationships with Interpol, for they very much needed what Interpol had to offer. The illicit drug traffic was then growing toward its present overwhelming dimensions; counterfeiting was on the verge of enormous growth; and there was an upsurge in the smuggling of gold and diamonds. The United States Secret

Service, the Bureau of Narcotics, and the Bureau of Customs found themselves severely hampered without contacts in foreign countries, and Interpol had the machinery to help them establish such contacts. Without Interpol's blessing, United States agents attempting to operate in foreign countries might at any moment find themselves suspect and subject to deportation or arrest.

Agents of those bureaus developed their informal "affiliations," and the Department of the Treasury is said to have contributed money to help meet Interpol's annual budget. But there were problems. One investigator generally didn't know what his compatriots were doing, and stories began to circulate of undercover men unwittingly investigating one another. Some old-timers were reminded of the Prohibition Era, when the department's revenue agents and members of the Coast Guard became involved in shoot-outs because one team would mistake another for a gang of smugglers or rum-runners. Such mix-ups are a recurring problem in governmental affairs, and the preventive measure is coordination. The secretary of the treasury had created a position in the department that was responsible for law-enforcement coordination.

In 1957 the man appointed to the new job was Myles J. Ambrose. One of Ambrose's first actions was to approach J. Edgar Hoover, asking his assent for the Treasury Department to take over the Interpol membership, which was dormant but still on the statute books. Hoover consented, and the original law was amended in 1958, permitting the attorney general to designate the secretary of the treasury as the official United States participant in Interpol and authorizing annual expenditures of up to $25,000, of which $11,000 constituted dues to the organization.

Eleven thousand dollars a year may seem a small financial contribution considering the value received. That much money was equivalent only to the wages of a couple of small-city policemen. For its $11,000, the United States was to receive continuous worldwide help in the suppression of smuggling, counterfeiting, and drug traffic, plus other law-enforcement assistance. At the time, however, the allocation seemed generous, for under the original statute the American contribution had been $1,500 per year.

In the ten years that followed, the annual United States dues contribution to Interpol increased to $28,500, equivalent to a fair-size retainer for an attorney defending a middle echelon crime boss in a narcotics violation case or equivalent to the import price of six to eight pounds of heroin, which, if successfully smuggled into the United States, makes 300,000 to 350,000 doses for illegal sales by dope pushers. In 1970 the American annual contribution increased to $48,000, and on January 1, 1973, it increased again, to $75,000. The significance of the increased contributions is that the United States had reestablished itself as a member of the organization of nations officially pledged to cooperate in the suppression of international crime—crime of which the United States had become one of the principal victims.

Ambrose left the Treasury Department in 1960 after the United States had returned as an official member of Interpol. He had served as leader of the United States delegation to the General Assembly meetings in 1958 and 1959. In 1960, with the national administration soon to change, Ambrose departed Washington and went to work as director of the Waterfront Commission of New York. Nine years later he was back on the scene as United States commissioner of customs, and in 1972 he was appointed a special assistant attorney general responsible for law-enforcement coordination against drug abuse, and again a delegate to Interpol conferences.

In 1960 Interpol held its annual General Assembly in Washington, D.C. At about the same time NBC television was presenting "The Man from Interpol" weekly. The American press flocked to the capital to see how closely the organization resembled the TV show. They were disappointed. The "boss" of Interpol himself failed to live up to the TV fantasy image of Inspector Duval, superdetective. Marcel Sicot, secretary general at the time, actually had had an outstanding career as a tough and brilliant police officer in France's Sûreté before assuming leadership of Interpol; he then had assumed the job of directing a complex global organization and nurturing its growth. As far as the American journalists were concerned, however, he was just another desk-bound executive. The TV version was much more exciting and glamorous.

An Interpol office was functioning in Washington during the 1960s, but most of the time the real-life American "man from Interpol" really had little more than a desk job. The United States membership had legitimacy, but the activities at the office handling it were limited. The action was overseas, where customs and narcotics agents continued their own individual professional contacts with foreign police officials who might be helpful to them.

In 1963 the United States Secret Service decided that it, too, ought to have resident foreign representation. Not only was counterfeiting abroad on the increase, but United States presidents were traveling abroad more and more to meet heads of state around the world, and the security of the chief executive is a Secret Service responsibility. An office was opened in Paris to handle matters in Europe, Africa, and the Near East. A short time later another office was opened in Honolulu to handle matters in the Far East. Even more recently, an office was established in Puerto Rico to cover South America. These outposts developed close, direct relationships with lawmen in each area.

There were about 40,000 separate municipal, state, and federal police departments in the United States, but no provision existed for any of them to follow through on investigations outside the country should the occasion arise. Nor was there any established system by which a foreign law-enforcement officer could gain access to these American police departments.

The approach of the United States to international crime contrasted sharply with that of other countries, where Interpol's national central bureaus acted as channels of communication for all sectors of their police agencies when investigation or prosecution was concerned with a crime that crossed national frontiers. Not that the spirit of cooperation was lacking in the United States; there simply was no effective machinery for communication. Austria, a small country, exchanged some 31,000 items of information with police forces of other nations in 1968, compared with a handful of such exchanges by the United States office.

Running the desk of Interpol Washington must have seemed like the world's least glamorous job. The bureau kept normal business hours, observing Saturdays, Sundays, and holidays despite the seven-days-a-week practices of the underworld. Relatively few domestic police inquiries for information came to the Interpol office in Washington, and relatively few inquiries came in from foreign police agencies. When foreign police did inquire, it took the office an average of over three months to respond. Customs, narcotics, and Secret Service investigations usually bypassed the American Interpol office and used the direct contacts they had developed abroad through their resident agents. The Washington bureau at that time was simply not operating as an effective liaison. By contrast, its counterpart in Rome assisted in the arrest of 205 persons wanted for crimes in other countries during 1968.

Ultimately the Americans began to catch on to the idea of regularized cooperation against international criminals. In 1969 Eugene T. Rossides, a New York lawyer, became assistant secretary of treasury for enforcement and operations. Many people thought of him as a former football star, but his career actually had included years of service in the rackets bureau of New York District Attorney Frank Hogan, and as an assistant attorney general for the state of New York prosecuting stock frauds.

Rossides started by introducing some small but basic changes on the United States side of the Interpol network. His least spectacular but most important move was to appoint a working investigator rather than an administrator as the bureau's chief. Kenneth S. Giannoules took the job with a ten-year background as a Secret Service agent; he was a field man rather than a desk man.

Another change took place on the communications front. Interpol Washington now has its channels open twenty-four hours a day, seven days a week, through radio, telex, telephone, and, in emergencies, through "hot line" telephone facilities. In December, 1971, it joined the radio network of Interpol.

In themselves these changes and new communications facilities may seem prosaic in the framework of Washington's vast bureaucracy, but with them came a new policy. The policy was to open international facilities to all law-enforcement agencies of the United States—local, state, and federal—in which a criminal investigation or prosecution is in progress. An assistant United States attorney in New York could now seek information in Istanbul by a telephone inquiry to Washington, and a Montana sheriff could pursue an investigation in Australia in the same way. The national central bureau in Washington would forward the inquiries to Istanbul and Sydney, respectively, and in each place the inquiries would be relayed to competent agencies for follow-through and action.

The goal is to regularize assistance to the nation's entire system of criminal justice. Not long ago a man convicted of sex and assault crimes in San Diego jumped bail and disappeared. Some time later, the police in Melbourne arrested four men, including a United States citizen, for burglary and theft. The four were convicted and sentenced. The Melbourne police as a routine matter sent information about the American burglar to Interpol Washington, where it was channeled to FBI files. The American offender, jailed in Melbourne under an assumed name, was found through fingerprint records to be the fugitive from San Diego. San Diego authorities were alerted, and the courts notified Australian officials that a bench warrant was out for the man. When he finished his sentence in Melbourne, the Australian police deported him to the United States, and San Diego authorities took over when the plane touched down in California.

This case in itself is not spectacular, and it was handled with routine machinery. The authorities did not have to unleash a massive manhunt to accomplish the purposes of criminal justice. Although differences of opinion and policy exist concerning the punishment or rehabilitation of offenders, society obviously can choose neither unless the offender in question has been caught. A manhunt may be a dramatic test of police capabilities, but it can only be used in selected instances, as in the search for the assassin of Dr. Martin Luther King, Jr. For day-to-day countermeasures against crime, the test of a crime-fighting organization is whether existing facilities at home and abroad can be employed efficiently and economically.

America's new interest in improving its control over international crime is symbolized by a row of telex machines in Room 1130 of the Treasury Department. The machines are plugged into the world network of Interpol. A message put into a similar machine in Istanbul will be received by the one in Washington, D.C., and be relayed to wherever it is needed in the American anticrime machinery. Messages also move in the opposite direction. Originally the principal link to the network, the telex now supplements radio.

The fact that America's interest in international cooperation has entered a new phase is becoming known around the world. The number of foreign police requests for assistance from American police in their criminal investigations has increased from a handful per year up to 1968 to more than 1,300 per year by mid-1971. The word has spread more slowly in the United States itself. Police organizations at all levels made about 200 requests in 1969 for investigative assistance from foreign police agencies; the number of those requests increased much less than foreign requests—to 700 per year by mid-1971.

Such requests, incoming and outgoing, are handled by the Interpol bureau of each foreign country that receives communications from the Interpol bureau in Washington. Each in turn receives and transmits the inquiries from and responses to the operating police official concerned with the particular cases, whether in the United States or in another country.

One reason for the attention the American Interpol office is receiving is the increased speed in its response to inquiries from abroad. By mid-1971 the response time of Interpol Washington had been cut from more than three months to an average of thirty days. Emergency cases, of course, are given priority and handled immediately.

Interpol Washington itself conducts no investigations. Its function is limited to facilitating the work of other police organizations by steering requests to the proper agency for information or action. Sometimes major cases are involved. Agents of the Narcotics and Customs Bureaus recently seized several smugglers and 750 pounds of hashish that they had brought to Boston from India. Instructions were passed via Interpol Washington to New Delhi, and police seized the other side of the gang with 150 pounds hidden in a Japan Air Lines office in that city. At other times a relatively small case sets the international machinery in motion. In Montgomery County, Maryland, a woman was robbed of her sole inheritance, a solitaire diamond. To dispose of the diamond, the thief had mailed it to a woman friend in Hong Kong. He was traced by local police and caught, and he pleaded guilty. But the diamond was gone. When he divulged what he had done with it, Montgomery County police requested assistance from Interpol Washington, which sent a cable to Interpol Hong Kong. The chief of the Hong Kong bureau requested the post office there to set a mail watch and to have local police call on the lady to whom the diamond was addressed. In a very short time, the diamond was on its way back to the Maryland woman.

A new development is the growing interest of nonfederal police agencies in cooperation with foreign police through the Interpol network. Before 1969 fewer than 80 inquiries a year came to Interpol from city, county, and state police; by mid-1971 these requests came at a rate of more than 200 a year. At the same time, nonfederal police departments were learning how to use Interpol's facilities. During 1971 the Netherlands Antilles asked Interpol Washington if it could obtain information about an American lawyer who had settled in their territory and was operating as a corporate financial expert. Interpol Washington distributed the inquiry. The prompt reply was that the man was a fugitive, wanted in Santa Anna, California, for theft, forgery, and fraud. He had been swindling elderly Californians and had extracted some $3 million from about 60 individuals. While Interpol Washington forwarded the identification to the Antilles, the prosecutor in Santa Anna obtained a federal warrant and requested through Interpol Washington that the Antilles have the man detained until extradition proceedings could be completed.

In addition to international cases from abroad and from American police, Interpol Washington has begun to handle a volume of intelligence work, with more than 800 cases a year coming to them from foreign police. Interpol forwards them to various agencies for inquiry and action.

In October, 1971, a seemingly routine intelligence report came to Interpol Washington from Interpol Beirut concerning three United States nationals who had been arrested after a quantity of hashish was discovered packed in an automobile that was to be exported to the United States via Pakistan. The suspects were reported to be natives of Portland, Oregon. Interpol Washington furnished a copy of the report to the Bureau of Customs office in Portland, where it was handed to one of the bureau's agents.

The agent began routine inquiries that grew into a major investigation: he discovered that Portland was being developed into a port of entry by drug smugglers who were hiding the drugs in foreign cars shipped by freighter. One result was the largest single hashish seizure in history—1,330 pounds packed in a Volkswagen truck—and countermeasures for blocking this channel.

Another result was a tip passed on to the Royal Canadian Mounted Police in Vancouver that led to the discovery that the same gang was using *two* freighter routes—Beirut-Pakistan-Portland and Beirut-Pakistan-Vancouver. The Mounties' investigation led to the seizure of 900 pounds of hashish hidden in a Volkswagen on the docks of Vancouver. Here, too, countermeasures were established. Interpol Washington has increased its intelligence liaison work from approximately zero in 1968 to more than 1,100 items of information a year channeled to the Bureau of Narcotics and Dangerous Drugs, the Bureau of Customs, the Secret Service, the Internal Revenue Service Intelligence Division, the Alcohol, Tobacco, and Firearms Division, and the Immigration and Naturalization Service.

Like any network of its kind, the Interpol system can operate effectively only if two-way communication is maintained. Interpol Washington is regarded as expert in certain specialties, such as American style organized crime. Recently Interpol Washington noticed, while sifting Treasury Department intelligence summaries, a routine surveillance report that two of Meyer Lansky's confederates were planning to join that Mafia notable in his new Israeli home. The information was channeled to Interpol Tel Aviv, and the Israeli intelligence service had agents at the airport to turn them back when they arrived. The Israeli government is said to have become quietly concerned about American crime syndicates establishing a base in their country through Jewish criminals who take advantage of their Law of Return. The new effectiveness of Interpol in this regard contrasts with the situation several years ago, when Lansky traveled to London to attempt development of arrangements for a Mafia foothold in England's then-new gambling industry. On that occasion Lansky walked through the airport checkpoint, conducted his business, and returned home completely unmolested by British police.

Interpol also entered the case of a South American crook who carried credentials of a captain in the Bogotá, Colombia, Police Department and established contacts with the New York City police. Through Interpol Washington, the New York police were able to learn that his credentials were fake and that the man actually was a notorious thief, forger, and swindler who had been convicted and sentenced, had escaped from prison, and was using the "police captaincy" as a disguise. The New York police were happy to avoid embarrassment and to assist their South American colleagues by having the fugitive shipped back home.

Frantic American parents year after year hear that their child has disappeared while traveling abroad alone or with a tour group. As Interpol becomes better known in the United States, it is probable that small-town police will start channeling anxious parental inquiries to the Washington unit of the network. For instance, during the summer of 1971 a twenty-three-year-old woman was reported missing from her tour group while traveling through England. Interpol London, acting at the request of Interpol Washington, traced the young woman and reunited her with her family.

Some young people from America have gotten into trouble overseas as drug offenders. By the summer of 1972, nearly a thousand American youths were in the jails of Europe, Africa, the Middle East, and Mexico. The Interpol network can help keep track of youthful drug offenders who get into trouble with the police in various countries around the world. Interpol intervention cannot bring about their release from jail, but it may sometimes be able at least to furnish information to the parents. Interpol may also come to have the unhappy responsibility of serving as a clearinghouse for the records of young Americans who become drug law violators abroad.

One of the strangest disappearance cases involving Interpol and the United States was the Utter and Forget case. On February 17, 1969, William James Wilson reported to the office of the district attorney of Los Angeles County that his wife, Norma Bell Carty Wilson, had disappeared somewhere in Europe or North Africa while on an alleged business trip with one Thomas Utter, who was also known as Thomas Devins. The trip concerned foreign investments in the United States.

Devins had returned from that trip in possession of $1 million worth of real property in Los Angeles County that had previously belonged to Wilson. According to Wilson, Devins had no plausible explanation for the disappearance of Mrs. Wilson, though Devins claimed that she had said something about going to Scandinavia for cosmetic surgery.

On the basis of the initial report, Investigator William R. Burnett, Jr., and Deputy District Attorney Stephen S. Trott launched an investigation to determine what had happened to Mrs. Wilson. When they determined that a number of other countries would be involved, they conducted the investigation through the facilities of Interpol.

As the investigation proceeded, the investigators learned that a Canadian citizen, Robert Forget, had accompanied Mrs. Wilson and Devins to Canada, Spain, and North Africa and then had returned from North Africa to Los Angeles via Paris, leaving Devins and Mrs. Wilson in Tangier. The investigation also disclosed a number of fraudulent land transactions in Los Angeles County made by Devins with Wilson as the victim.

On the basis of statements by relatives, airline and hotel records, and post cards, a partial sequence of events was pieced together: Mrs. Wilson and Devins, after a circuitous journey, arrived in Locarno, Switzerland; the next day Devins was in Geneva, but no trace of Mrs. Wilson could be found there.

At this point, Burnett and Trott set off on an odyssey. City by city, hotel by hotel, they followed the trail of Devins and Mrs. Wilson through New York, Madrid, Málaga, Torremolinos, Algeciras, Milan, Geneva, Zürich, Locarno, Genoa, and Lisbon. In each country, the Interpol bureau supplied assistance in the investigation. By the time the trail ran out in Geneva, Burnett and Trott firmly believed that Mrs. Wilson had come to a sad end between Locarno and Geneva during November, 1968.

When Burnett and Trott returned to the United States, they made contact with Forget, who was then residing in the state of Washington. It took several months to persuade him to talk, but he finally told the following story: He and Devins had originally gone to Europe as part of a scheme to release Moise Tshombe, former premier of the Republic of the Congo, who had been taken from a plane in Algeria and imprisoned there. Their reward was supposed to have been $25 million. En route they were joined by Mrs. Wilson in Montreal. According to Devins, Mrs. Wilson was coming along as part of a business venture that was not connected with the Tshombe plot.

When they got to Madrid, Devins told Forget that he was going to do away with Mrs. Wilson because she was about to discover that he had stolen land from her and her husband in Los Angeles County, and he had no wish to pay for his crime. Forget indicated an unwillingness to go along with the murder. Sometime after this, the three of them were arrested by the Málaga police on a weapons violation and released; shortly after they reached Tangier, Forget returned to Los Angeles. Moise Tshombe seemed to have been completely forgotten. A short time after Forget's return, Devins showed up in Los Angeles and told him that he had shot Mrs. Wilson in the head and that he had disposed of the gun, the body, and her mink coat in a place where they would never be found—a "perfect crime." He then gave Forget a nine-carat green stone that he said had come from Mrs. Wilson's ring.

Devins was arrested and charged with first-degree murder, armed robbery, and multiple counts of grand theft. A request was sent to member countries of Interpol in Europe to search for Mrs. Wilson's coat. In September, 1970, men from the Geneva Police Department found a cardboard box in a storage locker in a Geneva train station. Inside were not only Mrs. Wilson's mink coat but also her clothing, stained with blood in a way that indicated that she had, indeed, been shot in the head.

Devins went to trial in the fall of 1970. During the course of the trial numerous police officers and civilians from Europe went to the United States to testify for the prosecution. Their travel arrangements were carefully planned and coordinated by Interpol. After a three-month trial, Devins was sentenced to life imprisonment.

A novel aspect of this grotesque case is the part that the Interpol network played in making it possible for the Los Angeles district attorney to pursue the case to completion. The American investigators would have had great difficulty and might have been *personae non gratae* had they attempted to conduct their own investigation in any of the dozen countries they visited had Interpol not smoothed the way. Through Interpol they had people working for and with them in each country, tracing persons, finding evidence, and bringing witnesses to the United States to testify. The case stands out not merely on its own merits but for its contrast with the handling of the case of the five check-passers from South America who were apprehended in New York.

The increasing participation of the United States in Interpol comes not a moment too soon. As the world's wealthiest nation, the United States is a powerful magnet for criminals, both domestic and foreign. Until recently, international crime was largely invisible to the average citizen. Now, however, people are increasingly aware of the global scale of such offenses as counterfeiting, fraud against financial institutions, smuggling, stolen car rackets, and drug traffic.

What is not yet fully apparent to most citizens is that Interpol not only is an important ally in the struggle against international crimes such as these but offers the most effective defense against them.

7
Interpol
and Bank Fraud

E<small>VERY</small> day the banks of New York receive tens of thousands of letters from all over the world. On one particular Monday in April, 1964, six letters from Zürich, Switzerland, were received by the branches of five particular banks. One was addressed to the First National City Bank of New York, another was addressed to the Chase Manhattan Bank, two went to the Manufacturer's Hanover Trust Company, one to the Meadowbrook National Bank, and one to the Irving Trust Company.

All the five banks have South American depositors, and the six letters were from some of those depositors. Typical of the letters was the one received by the First National City Bank from Martin Otero, who was living in São Paolo, Brazil. It had been sent airmail from Zürich on the previous Friday, a seemingly routine request for the urgent transfer of $24,000 by cable from Otero's account at First National to his account, number M-538-0101, at the Bank of Rohner & Com-

pany in Zürich. (Names used in this chapter are mainly fictitious to preserve the privacy of persons who were actually involved.) The signature on the letter matched the one the bank
had on file, the funds were on deposit, and all the other details
were in proper form, so First National transferred the money
by cable.

Chase Manhattan's letter from Zürich was from Arturo
Nesner of Buenos Aires. It instructed the bank to transfer
$25,000 by cable from his account at Chase Manhattan to his
account, number 825-391-91N, at the Union Bank of Switzerland in Zürich. The letter was signed by Nesner. Again, the
signature matched the one on file at the bank, the request was
made out in proper form, and the funds requested were on deposit. Chase transferred the money by fast cable.

Manufacturer's Hanover, Meadowbrook National, and
Irving Trust received similar requests from Brazilian and Ar-
gentinian depositors, all in order, all for funds on deposit, all
with verifiable signatures; they all took similar action. By
Wednesday $96,000 had been cabled to six different banks in
Zürich. On Thursday and Friday someone visited each of the
Zürich banks and withdrew the deposits.

That was only the first wave. The second involved four
New York banks and began on Monday and Tuesday of that
same week. Three letters came to Chase Manhattan, two to
Manufacturer's Hanover, one to Chemical Bank, and one to
Grace National Bank. The letters had been mailed in Paris by
Brazilian and Argentinian depositors who all seemed to be
visiting Paris at the same time. Each urgently requested that
funds be sent by cable. The banks in New York, with one exception, followed instructions. By Thursday and Friday
$130,000 had been cabled and was on deposit in six Parisian
banks. On the following Monday and Tuesday, someone
visited each of the Parisian banks and withdrew the $130,000
in cash.

The exception was Manufacturer's Hanover Trust Company. One of the two letters it had received was from an Argentinian depositor named Bernardo Emler. It requested that $20,000 from his New York account be transferred to Account Number 44711 at the Banque Internationale de Commerce. Emler's account, however, had been very active, and the balance was too low to permit the transfer without overdrawing.

Emler is a wealthy businessman who lives in one of the most fashionable districts of Buenos Aires and has for many years maintained an account at Manufacturer's Hanover. Just before this incident, he had been subjected to a banking matter of some annoyance. Two checks he had written, each for $10,000, had not been delivered to the people to whom they were made out. When Emler became aware of this, he stopped payment on both checks and issued new checks that were delivered and collected. Now here was a puzzling cable from the bank referring to "his request" for the transfer of $20,000 to his account in Paris at the Banque Internationale de Commerce. The cable said that his balance was down to $13,000 and would he please advise them how to handle the matter.

Emler replied at once; he had no French bank account; he had not been out of Buenos Aires for a year; and he had most assuredly not requested the transfer of any dollar funds to Paris. In a follow-up letter, he referred to the two undelivered checks for $10,000 each. It now seemed that they might have been stolen from the mail by someone who had substituted a transfer order in the same amount in order to perpetrate a fraud through an agent in Paris. Emler notified the Buenos Aires police.

The third wave hit on the Wednesday of that memorable week. Manufacturer's Hanover received a letter from a São Paolo depositor named Juan Singlo Huerto, requesting the transfer of $19,000 to the account of Maria Leve at the Banque Lambert in Brussels. The letter had been mailed in

Brussels on Monday. The request was urgent and asked that the funds be transferred by cable. Manufacturer's Hanover honored the request. On the same day, three similar letters came from Brussels to Chase Manhattan, Irving Trust, and the Bank of Smithtown. The letters to Chase Manhattan and Irving Trust were honored at once, and a total of $35,000 was transferred to banks in Brussels, where, within a few days, someone again appeared and drew out the funds in cash. The Bank of Smithtown, however, was another exception.

A Long Island suburban bank, the Bank of Smithtown did not have many South American depositors. One of them was a local resident, a Baptist minister who had been assigned to missionary work in São Paolo and had continued his bank account in Smithtown. The letter from Brussels was ostensibly from the minister, the Reverend Harrison B. Russell, requesting the transfer of $10,000 from his account by cable to the account of Maria Leve. Like the other letters from Brussels, it had been mailed on Monday and received on Wednesday. The funds in Reverend Russell's account were awaiting the clearance of a newly deposited check. It would take ten days before the bank would transfer the $10,000 to the bank in Brussels. Since the Bank of Smithtown does not have its own foreign department, it asked Manufacturer's Hanover to handle the transaction. By that time Manufacturer's Hanover had learned that it had been the victim of forged foreign transfer requests. An officer of the bank suggested to the Smithtown bank that it get a verification for the transfer order.

Reverend Russell was a man of modest means. It happened, however, that his church elders had given him a special allotment of $14,400 in the form of a check that he had deposited in the Smithtown bank by mail. Though it seemed to take a little longer than usual, in due course Reverend Russell had received through the mail a deposit receipt from the bank. And then he received an astonishing phone call.

It was from the executive vice president of the Bank of Smithtown. He asked Reverend Russell about his trip to Belgium, about a letter he had sent them from Brussels, and about the transfer of $10,000 to Maria Leve. When the minister was finally convinced that his caller was serious, he informed the bank officer that he had never been in Brussels in his life, knew no one named Maria Leve, and had no intention of giving her or anyone else any of his church's money. In passing, he complained that the receipt for his deposit had been late. This puzzled the man in Smithtown, for the bank always mailed receipts on the day of deposit.

Thinking about it afterward, both the bank officer and the clergyman wondered how and why anyone should choose Reverend Russell as a target for bank fraud. Never before had he had so much as two thousand dollars in his account, but the moment a substantial sum had been deposited, someone in Belgium had almost succeeded in stealing it. The Interpol specialists who worked on this case began by posing questions and answering them on the basis of the little evidence available.

First, who would do such a thing? The perpetrator must be someone who had figured out a system for getting his hands on $261,000 painlessly in two weeks—$96,000 in Zürich, $130,000 in Paris, and $35,000 in Brussels.

Second, how many persons were involved? The letters, which supposedly had been written by seventeen different people, presumably strangers to one another and supposedly traveling in three different European countries, were worded almost exactly alike, something like this:

Gentlemen:

I herewith request you to make the following payment to the debit of my account with you:

TEN THOUSAND U.S. DOLLARS (U.S. $10,000) to the (*name of bank, address, city, country*) to be credited to my account in

that bank. Account No. ____. [Or to the credit of (*another name*), Account No. ____.]
Please make the transfer by telegram.
Thanking you in advance, I remain,

Very truly yours,

(*signature*)

There were other similarities as well. Each swindle had occurred in a cycle of from ten days to two weeks, reckoning from the day on which a group of letters arrived at the American banks until the day on which the cash was withdrawn from the European banks. Not only that, but the letters through which the fraud was carried out were typed on the same typewriter.

To make this scheme work, someone had to know the names of wealthy depositors, the names and addresses of their banks, and the sizes of their bank balances. Someone also had to obtain samples of their signatures and learn the reference codes identifying their accounts. In order to get such information, someone had to be able to intercept mail passing between the banks and their depositors without arousing suspicion.

The easiest way to do that would have been to buy the cooperation of a mail deliverer, preferably one who delivered in a well-to-do neighborhood in São Paolo, Montevideo, or Buenos Aires. Interpol investigators have uncovered several conspiracies that used this technique. It's quite simple to arrange. The conspirators simply find a letter carrier who delivers mail in the right neighborhood and who can use some extra cash each month. They arrange to meet him each day and go through his sack of mail. They remove certain letters, keep them overnight, and return them the next morning and go through the bag for more.

The next step requires a kettle of boiling water and some photographic equipment. The letters from the banks are steamed open and the canceled checks, deposit slips, and monthly statements are photographed. Then the letters are resealed and given back to the mailman for delivery, and no one suspects. The photographed material supplies the names and addresses of banks, account numbers, deposit information, code references for identifying the accounts, and signatures. All that remains to be done is to secure the services of a good forger.

Up to this point, the scheme sounds relatively simple— steaming open letters, taking photographs, developing and printing them, and copying signatures. This was obviously only part of the picture, however.

The scheme is tremendously complex. Bank accounts have to be opened in a number of foreign cities; deposits must be made; cash must be withdrawn; the movements of the numerous people involved must be coordinated; expenses must be paid and accounted for; the proceeds must be assembled and divided; and each activity has to be timed and carried out on schedule. And all the fake bank transfer letters must be signed by an expert forger. Even Interpol was impressed, particularly the people who work in Group D, whose special province was just such cases—bank fraud.

Bank thefts probably began as soon as the first bank opened about 2,500 years ago, although modern forms of bank fraud did not appear until the early Middle Ages. At that time bankers performed special services for merchants, as pirates and highway robbers made the transfer of cash by ship or overland a hazardous venture. Venetians bought from Alexandrians, Alexandrians from Persians, Germans from Venetians, and all were understandably wary of carrying or sending money for payment. An alternative to direct payment for goods was needed. The alternative became a system of "bills of exchange," by which Venetian merchants, for instance, kept money on deposit in Alexandria and gave or sent written orders to the holders of their deposits to pay out what they owed to those from whom they purchased.

This protected their money from pirates and highwaymen, but not, they soon learned, from people who were able to write. One Venetian forger of bills of exchange, for example, was so skillful and so prolific that at one time he paralyzed the entire banking system serving the merchants of Venice through bills of exchange.

Forgers at one time were dealt with harshly, but then more humane concepts of punishment developed, and the punishment for bank fraud was decreased. After all, it happened infrequently, since few people could write, and most of those who could were clerics. Moreover, the number of banking houses was small, limiting the scope and the effect of bank swindling.

As banking became more common, however, bank swindling became a more popular pastime, and as bills of exchange gradually developed into our modern system of paying by check, check forgeries and frauds took on more serious proportions. A formal check-writing system was in effect in the United States by 1681 in Boston, though it did not become general until the beginning of the twentieth century. It grew enormously after 1913, when the United States Federal Reserve System was established. By 1972, Americans were writing about 24 billion checks a year.

From time to time, some expert tries to determine the number of checks annually that are forged or that are otherwise fraudulent. Ten years ago, when only a few billion checks a year were written in the United States, it was estimated that forgers, swindlers, and other check manipulators were putting an average of one and a half million bum checks into the channels of finance each year. That was just about the time when the conspiracy that came to be known as the "South American Gang" was coming into existence, about two years prior to April, 1964, when those eight New York banks were taken for a financial sleigh ride.

The chief of Interpol's Group D kept an interesting wall

chart on this gang. Each important member was indicated by a plastic marker that was coded by number. His place in the criminal pecking order was signified by the position of his marker. As the details concerning the gang and its international operations were assembled piecemeal over the years in various countries and collated in the offices of Group D, and as the markers on the chart were moved about, a recognizable, logical picture began to emerge. It indicated Brazil as the country of origin and São Paolo as the headquarters city, where a man named Rick had lived before moving on to bigger and better things, and where a beautiful woman named Jannette had met a man named Osvaldo.

The list of the gang's members alternately grew and shrank as new names were added and as old ones were identified as aliases and eliminated. As the structure of the conspiracy emerged and the details were filled in, the role of each character became evident until, like a film scenario, the case could be broken down into leads, supporting players, and bit players. Eventually fitted in were the five people from South America who had been arrested for passing bad checks in New York in October, 1965.

Like a scenario, the plot had a number of subplots, making it one of the most complex operations in the annals of international crime. It was a scheme for the large-scale cashing of stolen traveler's checks and cashier's checks, for the systematic cashing of counterfeit cashier's checks, and for false transfers from the bank accounts of South Americans who kept money on deposit in North American banks. The important elements in the plan were volume of activity, continuity, speed, and change of pace. That meant employing agents who could handle bundles of counterfeit checks at one period, then switch to stolen genuine checks, then run through a series of interbank transfers, and then to bundles of stolen traveler's checks. It called for top-notch planning and intelligence work so that when the victims and police in one locality became aware of their activity, the organization could switch to another location or another kind of activity.

The operating teams were composed of couples. Almost every leading male member was matched with a female member, in each case an attractive woman who lived, worked, and traveled with him. Needless to say, there was no lack of male recruits.

As fresh evidence and facts came in, Interpol's telex machines and radios were busy sending and coordinating messages, transmitting circulations and bulletins. The headquarters in Saint-Cloud and the police forces of countries on three continents were in constant touch. Arrests were made, raids were executed, workshops were destroyed, printing plants were uncovered, suspects went to prison or were released for lack of sufficient evidence only to be rearrested, but parts of the organization surfaced again and again. As markers went up on the Group D chart, the corresponding names were processed. A growing crop of significant details emerged from the portrait parle, the analytic index, and the alphabetic file.

Long before Manera and his associates had come to the United States on that New York shopping spree, Interpol had had reports out on them and also on a woman named Jannette Polanski, known to be a member of the same gang. The fact that the reports made little impression in the United States and that Manera, Jannette, or their colleagues had probably entered and left the country at will many times before they were finally apprehended demonstrates the limits of the operations of Interpol Washington at the time.

Jannette Nemecek von Polanski, alias Maria Lucia Soarez, alias Rosanna Drago, was, according to police records, born in Prague on March 7, 1937. She never knew her father, and her widowed mother, remarried to a French ex-diplomat named André Mariotti, was living with Mariotti in Germany.

For the first ten years of her life Jannette lived with her paternal grandmother, Julia Stovok. When Mariotti died in 1946 Jannette's mother rejoined her and the grandmother, moving them to Paris and then to La Paz, Bolivia, where, as Eva Maria Mariotti, she managed a boutique.

When Jannette was fifteen, the family moved to Rio de Janeiro and then to São Paolo. Jannette's mother managed shops of various kinds along the way. In 1960 Jannette was twenty-three and extremely attractive, according to the Brazilian police. At about that time, her mother was implicated in a crime that had taken place in Germany fourteen years before and was extradited. Jannette said she was left in São Paolo with a lover and a child. She afterward told the Italian police that the lover was a Hungarian nobleman, Esterhazy von DeGalenta, who married her on his deathbed to give the child a name. (When she was arrested in Milan, a passport was found in her possession for Alexandra Anna Bella Esterhazy von DeGalenta, born in São Paolo on April 6, 1960.)

In September, 1963, so her story went, she got a job at the São Paolo Automobile Show, where she made friends with a handsome young man who called himself Raoul Martinez. Martinez told her that he was engaged in clandestine financial transactions and asked her to join him in Europe. They lived first in Marseille as Mr. and Mrs. Martinez, and then in Rome and then in Milan. It was he, she said, who involved her in bank fraud activities.

Jannette's story could be verified only to a point. The real story had to be pieced together from many sources, some of which are provided by the dossiers on her companions, principally Osvaldo Eneas Cocucci.

Osvaldo Cocucci, alias Raoul Martinez, alias Aristedes Gay Pellegrini, and alias many other names, was born on March 27, 1930, in Rio Quarto in the province of Córdoba, Argentina. Until well into his young manhood, he was a small-time crook working with others in forgery, counterfeiting, and check-passing rackets. When the police in his native country became too well acquainted with him, he moved on to Uruguay until police attention there induced him to go to Brazil.

In April, 1963, the Brazilian police exposed a large-scale counterfeit and fraud scheme based in São Paolo, and in a newspaper account of the case, Osvaldo Cocucci was given a one-line mention as a *pistolare*, or gunman. Little notice was taken when he dropped out of sight, but the next time his name appeared in the newspapers, two years later, it was as *capo* of a multinational organization that had engaged in swindles involving billions of lira.

Cocucci and Jannette, according to Italian police records, had been lovers in Brazil. She may, at that time, have been helping him in his criminal activities. Interpol Rio informed Saint-Cloud that she had been arrested in 1963 by the Brazilian police on a minor charge of false identity. When Cocucci became a major crook in Europe, he sent for her.

In Europe Cocucci worked his way up in the gang until he was in charge of European activities and given a share in the profits. At one point the Italian police listed him as the number-one man on their roster of the gang, but Interpol ranked him no higher than head of the gang's European operation. And, although he was not aware of the honor, he was so represented by a marker on the chart on the wall of the Group D office in Paris.

On the same chart was another marker that represented an Argentinian named Ricardo Roman Szuman, known to his friends and the police as Rick. Ricardo ("Rick") Roman Szuman was born in Buenos Aires on December 26, 1934. His father was a Polish diplomat assigned to Argentina. His mother, once a local beauty, had been married before. Rick's photographs show the cheekbones and facial structure of his Slavic inheritance combined with the dark eyes of the Latin. His boyhood was spent on the beaches around Montevideo. In his youth he was reported to be "in the lumber business" and then "in the import-export business," according to his mother, who was probably trying to cover up his real activities.

Rick was involved in the activities of his half brother by his mother's first marriage, Tadeo ("Dick") Roman Szuman. Dick Szuman is three years older than Rick. Starting at the age of twenty, Dick acquired a long Argentinian police record, mainly for theft, although in each instance he was released. In the 1950s he moved up from thefts to forgery and receiving and in 1960–61 transferred his activities across the bay from Buenos Aires to Montevideo. In 1961 he was jailed by the Uruguayan police for his part in a ring engaged in forging and passing stolen traveler's checks.

This caper was background for activity that was to follow. Shipments totaling $700,000 in First National City Bank of New York traveler's checks had been stolen from the mail at the Montevideo airport in January and February of 1960. A ring had been organized to get them cashed, and they were distributed across Europe and across the Pacific as far as Hong Kong and China. In December, 1961, the gang, including Dick, was apprehended, although Dick was listed as only "implicated."

Finding Uruguay inhospitable, Dick moved to Brazil, where he was soon involved in a similar scheme, this time counterfeiting as well as forging bank checks. Out of these schemes, which in themselves were not new ideas, Dick and his associates evolved the conspiracy that threw its tentacles around the world, ultimately involving hundreds of thieves, big and little, old pros and naive newcomers.

Monica Bach, for one, got into the act by chance. She was picked up on the Champs Elysée by Rick Szuman and grew so well into her role that for a time police thought she was a pivotal character. The other leading figures included Enrico Graziotti, the gang's master technician, an Italian forger and counterfeiter; Emilio Manera, alias Raul Domingo Geneyro, alias Armando Bisiani, and alias many other names, one of the New York Five; Wissocq-Bo, alias Peter Wichers, alias Jorge Washington Gonzales Ramos, also of New York Five; Carlos Arturo Cané, alias Enrique Weil, alias Carlos Sandro; and Teresa Federici, alias Maria Ipanien Taschian, alias Teresa Botti, also of the New York Five.

Among the supporting characters were Ingeborg Skoruppa, another pickup who never attained stardom; Juan Carlos D'Angelo Zuliani, who was teamed with Teresa Federici; Maria Elena Soyanes, a seventeen-year-old Uruguayan ingenue; and Bruno Briganzi, whose shadowy figure at one point took shape as the master plotter behind the whole scene. In the minor roles were people like Carmen Fuentes, Barcellos Garcia, George Campbell, Jacob Zorilla, Cesare Santos, and dozens of other small-time and apprentice criminals of all nations.

Most of these individuals had been known to the police of their native countries for some time, but the connection among them was concealed even after the existence of their international conspiracy was suspected. This fact, of course, was most important to the gang's success.

On June 9, 1963, a Señor Armando Bisiani flew to Geneva and checked into a modest and respectable hotel, the Jet d'Eau on the Rue du Simplon. As soon as he was settled in his room, he put through a call to Alfred Graf, a businessman in Lausanne. Bisiani had met Graf on a previous visit to Switzerland and had kept his name and phone number for future reference. Graf answered the phone, and he and Bisiani exchanged greetings and conversational amenities. In answer to Graf's query, Bisiani said that he was in Switzerland to buy gold for an associate in Buenos Aires for whom he was acting as an agent. He was paying in United States dollars. While they were on the subject, he asked whether Graf knew a reliable trader. Graf was only too happy to recommend his friend and colleague Albert Stauffer, whose office was located in Geneva.

Bisiani got in touch with Stauffer and told him that he was interested in buying twenty-five kilos of gold. The two men arranged to meet. During the meeting, Bisiani showed Stauffer a check that his principal, Cesar Bustamente, had provided for the transaction. It was a cashier's check for $28,000 drawn to his favor by the First National City Bank of New York at its Buenos Aires office, payable at the bank's New York City office on Wall Street. Stauffer was satisfied with the deal and pleased with his new customer. Why shouldn't he be? A trusted friend, Graf, had introduced Bisiani to him; Bisiani had shown him his passport and his money and had demonstrated a familiarity with European business methods. In showing his passport, Bisiani also allowed Stauffer to compare his appearance and signature with the photograph and signature on the passport. In fact, Bisiani gave Stauffer the First National check to take to his own bank for verification along with the customer's purchase order for the check. Issued in Buenos Aires, the check purchase order was the bank's record that it had received 3,175,144 Argentine pesos, the exchange rate on 28,000 United States dollars plus commissions.

Stauffer took Bisiani's check to his bank, the Swiss Bank Corporation, where it was verified and cashed. Stauffer then delivered twenty-five kilos of gold to Bisiani. The two men shook hands over the satisfactory conclusion of the deal and said goodbye. Bisiani returned to his hotel and checked out, leaving no forwarding address.

A week later Stauffer received a disturbing telephone call. Herr Kuntz of the foreign exchange department of the Swiss Bank Corporation told him that he had just received notice from the First National City Bank office on Wall Street that Bisiani's check had bounced.

"But you yourself verified it!" said the astounded Stauffer. The unhappy Kuntz could not deny it. All he could say in reply was that the message from First National said that the check had been stolen in blank in South America and that the Buenos Aires branch officer's signature was a forgery. The receipt for 3,175,144 Argentine pesos was also a forgery, and the Cesar Bustamente who was supposed to have made this payment to purchase the United States dollar check did not exist.

There were repercussions in several widely separated cities. In Geneva, Stauffer, officers of the Swiss Bank Corporation, and the local district attorney started a series of discussions to determine who was going to make good the $28,000 loss. The Swiss police took down full particulars of the crime, and in due course Interpol Zürich relayed the information to Interpol Paris.

In São Paolo the gang insiders were jubilant. Bisiani's trip had been a test run for their check-cashing scheme, and the system worked. In each instance the swindle would be transacted some five thousand miles away. The insiders would be even further insulated from detection when they could stay away from the scenes of the crimes. For instance, it was Stauffer who went to the bank to get the check cleared and who exchanged the proceeds for Bisiani's gold. If this could work in every case, the system would be perfect, for with an intermediary in the exposed position, the crook could keep his distance and, if need be, walk away from the scene should anything go wrong.

In New York officials of the First National City Bank put agents to work on a lengthy search for Bisiani all over Europe and South America; at one point, and unknown to them, he was sitting in a New York jail cell ten blocks from their Wall Street office. Bisiani was, of course, Manera, who had used the name Geneyro in New York.

After the Bisiani gold caper, Rick was put in charge of the European activities and told to move into full operation. Rick had been in Paris since 1962. He had been living unostentatiously with a mistress at 49 Rue Lacepede in the heart of the Latin Quarter. Bank officials with whom he conducted his "business" remember him as tall and well dressed with dark hair, a small moustache, and an olive complexion. He spoke French, English, and fluent South American Spanish. He looked every inch the stereotype of a "South American businessman." Bank officers invariably described the men who victimized them as looking like "typical South American businessmen."

Among his neighbors, Rick was regarded as unobtrusive and very pleasant. He paid his rent regularly and dressed well but not too well. He often slept all day and went out at night.

Toward the end of July, 1963, Rick made a trip to Germany and returned to the Rue Lacepede apartment with a new girl, one whom the Parisians of the neighborhood described as "nice-looking for a foreigner." The Paris police later described her as "very sexy." The new girl was Monica Bach, who met Rick on the Champs Elysée in what Americans call a "pickup" and Europeans call an "encounter." Monica was in a drugstore phone booth making a call, and Rick was waiting to use the phone. They began talking. She was from Germany and was on her way to Le Havre to see her German boyfriend. They parted and went their separate ways, but they arranged to meet again. When Monica returned to her home in Cologne, Rick went there for a visit. When he returned to Paris, she was with him, and the two began living together in Rick's apartment.

In August, like all good Parisians, they left the city for the Côte d'Azur, where they occupied an apartment in San Maxime. Living nearby was Emilio Manera in an apartment that he had taken for himself, his wife, and his teen-age daughter. Rick and Manera went over their plans. When their vacation was over, Manera took his family back to Milan and returned to San Maxime alone. George Campbell, a Canadian nicknamed "Ingles," joined the little group of conspirators, and a small but constant stream of "friends" dropped in to see them. At the end of August, Rick, Monica, Manera, and Campbell left San Maxime for Paris. The scheme was now set. Counterfeit bank drafts were to be mailed from Brazil at precise times. Each member of the team had to be in a particular city and at a specific bank at a precise time. Each team had to be ready to leave their location on completion of the scheduled swindles at a certain time, and the cash had to be securely transferred under the conspirators' control.

On September 1 the first "swindle brigade" moved out. Monica was sent ahead to Munich to "visit her mother," and Rick joined her a few days later. Manera went to Cologne. On September 6 Rick and Monica left Munich for Cologne and checked into the Hotel Carlton as Señor and Señora Julio Gedad Lestido of Asunción, Paraguay. They had passports in those names for identification. Manera had already checked in as Luis Albani, followed shortly by two more men with passports that identified them as Miguel Pardo and Carlos Pacheco.

The plan was to hit four banks in each of three cities— Cologne, Düsseldorf, and Bonn—and then return to Paris. It would take ten days in Cologne, the first city, to carry out the mission, then less time in the other cities because of the experience gathered in Cologne. To get around each city and to travel from city to city, three automobiles would be used, a Volkswagen belonging to Monica and two cars rented by Rick and Manera.

On the morning of September 9 the four men went into action. Attired as South American businessmen, with sets of identifying documents, including passports and international driver's licenses, each went to call on the manager of one of the selected banks, which included the Dresdener Bank, the Bankhaus Herstatt, the Bankhaus fuer Gemeinwirtschaft and the Commerzbank.

Each introduced himself and explained that he wished to

open an account, as he was developing a new business in the Cologne area. In each instance the new customer opened his account with some cash and said that foreign checks would be deposited by mail from abroad. Naturally, he would draw upon the checks only after they had cleared. He or his secretary would telephone to inquire.

Several days later a teller in the marble and bronze Dresdener Bank on Cologne's main shopping street peered out of his cage at a very attractive red-haired woman displaying a "well-endowed physique," as he later told the police. She identified herself as private secretary to Señor Julio Lestido, in whose account there had been deposited a few days earlier several checks drawn on the Schweizerische Kreditanstalt of Berne on the First National City Bank of New York, on the Commercial Bank of North America in New York, and on the New York office of the Swiss Bank Corporation. She had telephoned earlier to learn whether the checks had cleared and had been told that they had. Lestido, she said, wished now to draw out the cash.

The woman pushed a check signed by Lestido across the counter, accompanied by a letter of authorization on Lestido's business stationery instructing the bank to pay her the cash. The documents seemed to be in order, and the teller took them to the records cabinets to verify them. Then he went to the large, ornate safe in the security room and came out with packages of currency totaling 219,000 deutschmarks—about $55,000 in American money. The woman handed him a stylish leather bag, and he stacked the packages in it. He handed her the bank's receipt. She signed it, and he compared the signature with that on her passport. The teller then summoned a bank usher to assist her. The usher escorted her to the door and, at her request, accompanied her to the street. A Porsche was waiting at the curb with its motor running, a dark-complexioned man at the wheel. The usher handed in the bag and held the door for the woman as she slid into the seat beside the driver. He shut the door; she smiled her thanks; and the Porsche slid out into the stream of traffic.

That night the woman and her driving companion were in Düsseldorf, where they were joined by Manera, Pardo, and Pacheco. After a repeat performance in the new theater of operations, the brigade went on to Bonn, where they went through the routine again, presumably with even greater finesse after their practices in Düsseldorf and Cologne. It was in Bonn that Manera picked up a waitress named Ingeborg Skoruppa. He brought her with him when the entire crew returned to Paris at the beginning of October and moved into the Hotel Degli Stati Uniti near Gare St. Lazare with her.

Rick and Monica returned to the Rue Lacepede, where they were visited shortly after by Barbara von Wickenhagen, a Polish-born beauty in her early twenties who had come in from Brazil to pick up Dick Szuman's share and carry it back to him in São Paolo. By then, the police of seventeen countries were looking for the swindlers.

The checks in Lestido's name had begun to bounce in Cologne, as did those of his companions, and the banks had learned that Lestido, his secretary, and the other South American businessmen had disappeared. The Cologne police were notified, their commercial frauds section began to investigate, and the first reports were received shortly at the West German Interpol bureau in Wiesbaden.

On October 3 Dr. Paul Dikopf, chief of the West German Interpol bureau, initialed a form, and in the communications room a telex operator began to finger the keyboard of one of the machines. Simultaneously, at Interpol national central bureaus in seventeen countries, there appeared on the board tape of their machines the following telex message:

FROM INTERPOL WIESBADEN TO INTERPOL ZONES ONE AND TWO AND LEGAL ATTACHE AMERICAN EMBASSY BAD GODES-BERG—THE FOLLOWING INTERNATIONAL SWINDLERS WORKING BY MEANS OF CHEQUES HAVE COME TO NOTICE OF COLOGNE POLICE:

LESTIDO, JULIO, ABOUT 40, TALL, DARK, SHORT CUT HAIR ROUND
FACE DARK RIMMED SPECTACLES SPOKE GOOD ENGLISH "BLOOD"
DIAMOND RING LITTLE FINGER LEFT HAND PARAGUAY PASSPORT
7562 ISSUED 10 JAN 63; ALBANI, LUIS, ABOUT 40, SMALL, DARK,
WAVY HAIR ROUND FACE SPEAKING SOME FRENCH AND A LITTLE
GERMAN PARAGUAY PASSPORT 5243; PACHECO, CARLOS, SAME
DESCRIPTION AS FIRST SUSPECT PARAGUAY PASSPORT 5213;
PARDO, MIGUEL SAME DESCRIPTION PARAGUAY PASSPORT 4623.

There followed a lengthy description of the modus operandi
that the Szuman Mancra team had conducted in Cologne con-
cluding with

PLEASE ADVISE IF SIMILAR OFFENSES HAVE BEEN COMMITTED
LATELY IN YOUR COUNTRY.

Two weeks later, the West German Interpol bureau was on
the line again, this time adding a significant clue:

FROM INTERPOL WIESBADEN TO INTERPOL ZONES ONE AND TWO
AND LEGAL ATTACHE AMERICAN EMBASSY BAD GODESBERG—REF.
COLOGNE SWINDLE—IN FIFTH CASE ONE OF SWINDLERS WORKING
BY MEANS OF CHEQUES OPENED ACCOUNT IN NAME OF GOMEZ,
ROBERTO, AGE ABOUT 45, THICKSET, ROUND FACE, BLACK HAIR
SPANISH AND BROKEN ENGLISH.

It then spelled out further details of various transactions by
which the group had executed its maneuvers. Then it made reference to the team's female member:

ON 18 SEPTEMBER UNKNOWN WOMAN INQUIRED BY TELEPHONE
WHETHER ABOVE CHEQUES WERE CREDITED TO GOMEZ ACCOUNT.

Thus Monica Bach became the first weak link in the chain,
and for several months much of the multinational search
focused on her. In the meantime, with the police of half of
Europe looking for them, the organization brought down the
curtain on the first act of the swindle brigade and staged an
entr'acte.

On October 10 Arturo Riocama, a director of the Banko

Comercio de Chihuahua in Mexico, mailed a check for 100,000 United States dollars to his son in São Paolo. On October 20 a man who claimed to be Arturo Riocama, Jr., checked into the Hotel Continental just off the Place de la Concorde in Paris. He carried a Uruguayan passport bearing his photograph and the name Arturo Riocama, Jr. The next morning, he went around the corner to the Chase Manhattan Bank branch on Rue Cambon and said that he wished to open an account. He deposited $9,500 in German marks and United States dollars and a check drawn on a Mexican bank for $100,000 in United States currency. He accepted the fact that he would have to wait for the check to clear and asked the bank to notify him when it had. He let it be known that he was in the cattle business and that his home office was in Montevideo. He also rented a safe-deposit box and received a checkbook.

During the next few days he drew a few small checks on his account. During that time the bank was in touch with its New York office, asking it to verify the big check. On October 23 the New York office cabled that there were sufficient funds on deposit in New York, and that the signatures were good. That same day the Paris branch phoned the younger Riocama at his hotel, and that afternoon he called at the bank to get his money. An assistant manager of the bank suggested that he take it in the form of a check drawn on the Banque de France, which is insured against theft, but he preferred cash francs. The bank accepted his check for 450,000 francs and counted out the bank notes. The man accepted the fat packet of notes, thanked the bank employees who had waited on him, and made a leisurely exit from the bank. That was the last they saw of him.

On Thursday, October 31, Arturo Riocama, Senior, notified the bank in Chihuahua, Mexico, that the check he had sent his son was lost. The next day the canceled check arrived at the Mexican bank as a paid item from Chase

Manhattan. Back went a telegram to Chase Manhattan saying that the endorsing signature of the payee did not look authentic and advising Chase not to honor the check. It was good advice but it came too late.

In December a rental agency found an apartment for Rick and Monica at 63 Rue de Chezy in Neuilly, a fashionable, middle-class section of Paris close to the Bois de Boulogne. By this time, Interpol's Group D had been busy putting together a number of seemingly unrelated details coming in to them from Germany, Paris, South America, and New York. By adding and moving markers about on their chart, they were beginning to understand at least part of the developing scenario and see through at least some of the multiple identities.

As soon as Dick Szuman knew that the swindle was working, he sent Cocucci to Europe. Cocucci, in turn, sent for Jannette and joined her in Paris. In mid-November Dick Szuman hatched a new, larger scheme and was anxious to get it started. It would have to wait a short while, however. On New Year's Eve, he waved *bon voyage* to Maria Elena Soyanes, the seventeen-year-old daughter of one of his women friends. He was sending her from São Paolo to France on the *S.S. Provence* with a trunk full of bank drafts, checks, passports, and traveler's checks. In Paris, Rick met her and found her a place to live. Early in February, 1964, an informer's tip led detectives of the Paris division of the Sûreté to arrest her and take her into custody. Her suitcases were found to contain forty passports—German, French, Belgian, Austrian, Paraguayan, and Uruguayan—stacks of First National City Bank of New York cashier's checks, and traveler's checks.

Meanwhile, Monica had made a trip to Brazil to meet Rick's mother and to bring Rick's brother, Dick, two large briefcases stuffed with cash. When she returned, she went back to Rome instead of to Paris. Maria Elena Soyanes was in custody, and the hunt was too close for comfort in France. For some reason, Monica had not been provided with a false passport. Perhaps because it was her first visit to Italy, the masterminds had thought it unnecessary to furnish her with a false identity. At any rate, it was a bad slip. Improvisations in a well-rehearsed work can prove disastrous. Interpol had a wanted bulletin out on her. On February 26 the Rome police found her through a routine hotel register name check and went to her hotel on the Via Veneto to make the pinch. With her, they found a man unknown to them, for Rick Szuman had joined Monica.

When Monica answered the knock at the door, the police walked in. Aside from his accomplishments as an international crook, Rick Szuman was a very talented actor. He haughtily identified himself as a diplomat and produced a diplomatic passport. He confessed to having an assignation. The officers were extremely apologetic at having interrupted him at such a moment, but their orders regarding his companion came from a high official in the ministry. "His Excellency" graciously deferred to their pursuit of duty, expressed his regrets to the *signorina*, and withdrew. The wanted notice had mentioned only a woman.

The Italian police never got a second chance at Rick. He operated in Europe from the winter of 1962 to the spring of 1965, and in all that time the incident in Rome was the only time he ever was in danger of arrest.

"You cannot blame the police officers," said Major Orentini of the Rome Squadra Mobile. "The Interpol bulletin specified that only the woman was wanted. There was no cause to hold the gentleman. Our men were indeed quite efficient."

Monica was sent to a women's prison outside Rome. Word of her capture was flashed on the Interpol circuit. Investigators from Paris, Zürich, and Wiesbaden flew in to join Italian police in her interrogation. She was questioned during the first two weeks of March. In the meantime extradition formalities were being completed by the German Ministry of

Justice, and on April 9 Monica was on her way under tight security to Germany.

Monica proved to be cooperative. Interpol received reports on the information she gave. The international police organization and all European police agencies now had access to a detailed picture of how the South American swindle ring operated. In the meantime, however, the ring had established a new and bigger secret enterprise.

The new system was being organized before Monica was arrested. Enrico Graziotti, master technician in counterfeiting and forgery, was the key man. Through a man named Perez, he was recruited in Milan by Cocucci, using the name Umberto, and checked out by Rick Szuman, who flew from Paris under assumed identity for the interview. Then a new man came into the picture, a South American who called himself Riccardo. Riccardo was Dick Szuman's personal representative. He checked out and verified the arrangements that had been made so far and put Graziotti back in touch with "Umberto" Cocucci, who had money for the purchase of equipment and supplies.

Cocucci turned over to Graziotti 5 million lire in cash as an advance against expenses. He was to be paid 8 million lire for this stage of the work, plus a share of the profits. There was to be a chain of "factories," or workshops, mass-producing counterfeit financial paper and the documents necessary to convert the phony paper into good money. If one workshop were discovered by the police, the others would keep working. Each workshop was to have equipment that could be packed in an automobile or station wagon and moved to a new location in case the police closed in. The products were to be stored in various locations and moved periodically to prevent discovery. Small teams of check-passers would be supplied from each location, and new production would keep up the inventory.

Graziotti's first assignment was to produce 3,000 First National City Bank of New York bank checks in denominations ranging from 500 to 50,000 United States dollars and 1,000 bank checks of the Geneva branch of Intra Bank in denominations from 500 to 10,000 United States dollars and from 1,000 to 10,000 Swiss francs. He would be supplied with a set of genuine checks of each kind to copy. He also had to produce 500 international driver's licenses and 500 passports for the check-passers to use as identification. The passports would be Chilean, Peruvian, and Portuguese. Riccardo had authentic passports for him to use as models.

Since he was too well known in Milan, Graziotti set up his first workshop in Turin. He continued to live with his girl friend, Elena di Reda, in Milan and commuted to Turin. Cocucci moved from Paris with Jannette and rented an apartment in Rome. At intervals Cocucci went to Milan to meet with Graziotti.

When Monica was arrested in Rome, Cocucci and Jannette moved to Milan. They lived there until the Turin "factory" was operating smoothly. Then both Cocucci and Graziotti found apartments in Turin and moved there with their women. All this took place during the first part of 1964. By midyear the factory was turning out finished goods. Only Riccardo and Graziotti were allowed inside. At first the entire production was consigned to an Argentinian, Carlos Cané, and a Palestinian, Jacob Maracchlian, who carried the material to Rome and distributed checks and fake passports to three others, Zorilla, Pacho Baccaro, and Cesare Santos, who were to do the actual passing. Everything was very businesslike. Riccardo received $13,000 at the first delivery, of which he paid $8,000 to Graziotti. For the second batch of checks and passports Riccardo received $10,000, which he divided equally with Graziotti. He then gave Graziotti another 3 million lire to complete payments on the equipment.

Riccardo passed the word to branch out. Graziotti set up a workshop in Rome, where he and Cocucci rented furnished apartments, although each retained his apartment in Turin.

In October fate dealt Cocucci and Jannette a bad hand. Jannette, using the name Rosanna Drago, and Cocucci, using the name Aristedes Gay Pellegrini, and another couple, Carlos Cané, using the name Enrique Weil, and his mistress, using the name Carmen Fuentes, flew to Beirut, where they carried out a plan of cashing bank drafts at the Belgian Bank of Lebanon, the Sussex Bank, and the Middle East Bank. They also bought gold bars for smuggling. On the way to Damascus in a rented car, they were stopped at the Syrian frontier, and Jannette was detained.

According to an Interpol staff member in Rome, it was her beauty that proved her downfall. A bank teller in Lebanon became enamored of her and made a note of her address. Bemused by an uncontrollable attraction, he went to call on her after banking hours and discovered that the address was false. Frustrated, the teller anonymously tipped off the police. The police, in turn, set up a border watch and found that her identification documents were forged. She spent three and a half months in prison before she was released on bail of $15,000. She was required to remain in Beirut until her trial, but an agent sent by Cocucci got her out of the country on a false passport.

Back in Rome, she found that her baby daughter and her grandmother had been brought from South America to be reunited with her. The incident in Lebanon, however, had brought her to the attention of Interpol, and her file began to grow. Interpol Beirut reported to Interpol headquarters that she personally had extracted from $50,000 to $60,000 in cash from Beirut banks in two days, using bank drafts of the First National City Bank of New York and Intra Bank. According to the evidence that later was presented when she was tried in absentia in the Lebanese courts, it seemed that at least seven banks had been victimized by her for a grand total of $73,000 in about forty-eight hours. Some investigators were so impressed that they called her "Queen of the Forgers," and one newspaperman announced that she was the mastermind of the gang.

This brush with the authorities did not limit Jannette's capability. In time, banks and shopkeepers in a number of countries came to meet her by a variety of names and as a native of Argentina, Bolivia, Chile, Poland, Peru, Austria, Germany, France, and Brazil.

In the meantime on the other side of the Atlantic, the American Bankers Association was warning its members about the bank transfer swindle, and the International Air Transport Association, meeting in Montreal, was forming a Fraud Prevention Group to fight an international ring of ticket swindlers. Pan American World Airways had lost $200,000 through stolen ticket manipulations carried out at a travel agency in Buenos Aires, and Monica Bach's name had turned up on a ticket for a flight from South America to Rome. The ticket was from the batch swindled at the Buenos Aires travel agency.

In New York the representatives of eighteen banks and insurance companies that had incurred losses totaling $363,000 due to a rash of bank transfer swindles met to exchange views. The police were not invited, nor were they informed of the discussion. A proposal to investigate and prosecute the persons responsible at an estimated cost of about $20,000 was tabled.

European police were at a loss to understand the apparent complacency of American banks. Banks on both sides of the Atlantic were being victimized. In Europe the banks promptly notified the police. In the United States the banks seemed to practice a unanimous policy of silence. The only complaints they filed were at the Post Office Department.

In Paris, Interpol investigators were discussing a beautiful woman with red hair who had mysteriously appeared at banks in widely separated cities on the same day. On other occasions there was a brunette, then a blonde. In each instance the woman had withdrawn cash from fraudulent accounts or had cashed forged, stolen, or counterfeit bank checks. Ultimately, someone caught on. Usually two teams worked together, each comprising two couples traveling in two or three automobiles. The four women all wore similar dresses and wore duplicate wigs. Since bank tellers afterward in different cities seemingly described the same woman to police, it was obvious to the Interpol investigators that the women dressed to look alike.

The gang's performance was impressive. In the same month in which bank transfer capers were conducted against banks in Zürich, Paris, Brussels, and Antwerp, $37,500 in traveler's checks was stolen in the Montevideo airport. The checks were delivered promptly to the gang in Paris, and four people set off at once. The expedition swept through several German cities, cashing all the checks in ten days. Before this team was back in Paris, George Campbell was out with a team on a two-week check-cashing trip through Switzerland, passing phony checks worth 420,000 Swiss francs.

During June, 1964, Graziotti started to dismantle the Turin factory. The gang had become too big and perhaps too conspicuous. Distributors were meeting passers in bars and motels to give them the phony checks, passports, and driver's licenses. Large numbers of South Americans gathering frequently in a city like Turin were bound to draw attention. Rome would be safer.

Graziotti found apartments for the workshops in Rome and had the equipment trucked in from Turin. The South American contingent of the gang were recruited individually and sent to check in with Rick Szuman. He found them places to stay until they were assigned to a group supervisor and supplied with checks and passports. Each paid 25 percent of the face value of the checks to the organization and then divided the proceeds of his check-passing with his supervisor.

For example, a Paraguayan named Miguel Morinigo checked into a hotel in Rome. After a few days he made contact with Rick Szuman and moved to an apartment maintained by Rick for the purpose. There he met his supervisor,

Guido Miguel. Morinigo paid his expenses with $2,000 he had brought with him from South America.

A Mexican citizen, Jose Pedro Juarez, employed by an American petroleum company, caught wind of the scheme. With $2,000 saved out of his wages, he came to Europe as a tourist in December, 1964. In Paris he made contact with gang members at their hangout, the Café Fouquet on the Champs Elysée, and was referred to a contact in Rome. His deal was to negotiate Bank of America traveler's checks and to keep 30 percent of the face value for himself. On another occasion, he was sent on a tour of Swiss banks with a Belgian passport and $3,700 worth of City Bank traveler's checks. His compensation on that occasion was a flat $1,000.

Interpol eventually estimated the overall strength of the gang at about one hundred. At its heart was a central core of about thirty, including the girl friends of individual men. The South American contingent was supplemented by European crooks of various kinds. Some picked the pockets of tourists to obtain traveler's checks; others pilfered official stamps from minor civil service offices; and others burglarized town halls for identification cards in quantity.

The volume of activity was enormous. By the spring of 1965, Graziotti had three factories going full blast in Rome. Another was operating in São Paolo. The women, when not helping on bank transfers, were sent out to cash traveler's checks at shops, hotels, travel agencies, and railroad stations. Carlos Cané led a team into Nigeria and swindled banks in Lagos. Plans were laid for an expedition into India and Pakistan. Then, boldest of all, they decided to operate in the United States.

In March, 1965, a team flew into John F. Kennedy Airport, rented a Hertz car, drove to Philadelphia, and spent several days passing stolen traveler's checks. Later that month they began a really big move, an $850,000 bank transfer to be conducted in the heart of New York's financial district.

At first the maneuver went off like clockwork. In New York on March 31, April 1, and April 2, the team opened checking accounts at five banks in the Wall Street area. At the same time a team in Zürich opened an account at the Vontobel Bank of Switzerland. Between April 2 and 6 a third team in Buenos Aires mailed out more than one hundred checks drawn against the Banco Popular to twelve banks in New York. They were actually fraudulent bank drafts instructing the twelve banks to transfer funds to the gang's fraudulent accounts at the first five banks. By April 6 more than $850,000 had been transferred and was on deposit.

The New York team then instructed each of the five banks to transfer sums of money from their accounts to the account of the Zürich team in the Vontobel Bank. The instructions were in the form of bank transfer drafts. The banks began to comply. By April 21 almost half a million dollars had been deposited in the fraudulent account in Zürich.

At this moment, however, a small counterstroke was in motion. Interpol had been working on the problem for over a year with the police in various countries. Police had been advised to alert bank officials to the gang's techniques and to respond promptly. An assistant manager at the Vontobel Bank had gotten the message. When almost half a million dollars deposited by cable transfer suddenly flowed into a new account, he became suspicious and put a temporary freeze order on the account. His discreet inquiries led two of the New York banks at the other end to do likewise. The gang learned of the freeze orders, hesitated, and backed away. Their $850,000 caper had fizzled out.

At the same time Interpol was directing another counterstroke in Italy. It began on a Thursday, April 8, and brought results the following Sunday. On Thursday the proprietor of a small auto rental agency in the San Giovani section of Rome handed over to the patrolman on the beat a package containing ten passports—nine Chilean and one Peruvian. He had found them in the glove compartment of a Fiat 600 that he had rented to a foreigner named Julio O. Salinas.

Salinas had come to the agency accompanied by another man and a woman, also foreigners. He presented a Peruvian passport and an international driver's permit issued in Brussels and gave a Rome address. After a few days the agency tried to get in touch with him to find out how long he planned to keep the car and learned that Salinas was unknown at the address he had given. Then a report came in that the car had been seen in the neighborhood and that it was parked on the Via Acaia. The agency's proprietor went there, found the car, and drove it back to the garage. In checking it over he found the ten passports in the glove compartment. That afternoon the three foreigners returned to the agency to complain and asked for the package. They were told that it had been turned over to the police.

A police undercover agent combed the Via Acaia and learned that two South American men answering the descriptions furnished by the auto rental agent were tenants in an apartment there. The porter of the building said that they had described themselves as an engineer and a lawyer. On Saturday night a search warrant was issued. The next morning two detectives from the Squadra Mobile entered the apartment. They reported finding a large quantity of materials used to manufacture fake documents, including 77 completed passports of 10 different nations with identifying entries for various individuals, many with photographs; 103 blank passports of Peru, Portugal, and Chile; 4,132 unbound blank passport pages of those countries; 48 ID cards and 10 driver's permits, all Italian; 12 Belgian international driver's permits; 4,518 cashier's checks of Intra Bank and First National City Bank of New York with imprints of their branches in Milan, Geneva, San Juan, and London; 67 cashier's checks and traveler's checks of the Italian and Foreign Credit Institute; 210 cashier's checks of the Bank of Sicily; 7 credit cards; a large number of photographic negatives for passport pictures and for the reproduction of passport components; about 200 metal and rubber stamps carrying the insignia of the embassies and consulates of 14 countries for stamping entry and exit visas at airports and border frontier points and for stamping amounts onto bank checks in the sums of 10,000, 25,000, and 50,000 dollars; 1,824 packets of Credit Institute traveler's checks; and presses and other equipment for making and validating counterfeit documents.

It was estimated afterward that the cashing of the phony bank instruments would have resulted in losses to the banks involved totaling between two and three billion lire. The prize, however, was the collection of photographs for the phony passports. Together with the collection of negatives, they gave the police an illustrated guide through the Italian underworld. By Sunday night police squads were making arrests all over Rome, and Interpol Rome was issuing instructions to the Squadra Mobile units of Milan and other cities. Police units were alerted at airports and border crossings, and a series of bulletins was released to Interpol bureaus in Paris, Zürich, Wiesbaden, London, Vienna, and other cities.

The international character of the South American Gang was now revealed. Among the first fifty offenders arrested were nineteen Italians, eleven Argentinians, three Germans, three Spaniards, three Peruvians, two Czechs, two Mexicans, and one person each from France, Austria, Belgium, Egypt, Palestine, Paraguay, and Brazil.

Interrogation of those arrested in Rome and Milan quickly established that none of the leaders of the organization had been taken. Cocucci, who learned promptly of the setback, telephoned one of his people, a man named Agostinelli, in Bologna. Agostinelli found a basement in which to set up a new workshop and found a furnished apartment for Graziotti and Elena.

After that it was like a game of chess, with each side trying to checkmate the other. On Monday, April 12, the Rome police cleared out the apartment on Via Acaia. On Tuesday

Cocucci's man Zorilla backed up a station wagon down the street on Via Acaia, cleared out a factory from the top floor, and drove the equipment and supplies to the new workshop in Bologna. Cocucci, who had moved from Rome after Monica's arrest, was living in his Milan apartment with Jannette, the baby, and the grandmother. He still had his Turin apartment in reserve. The loss of the Rome installations was offset by new workshops in Milan as well as in Bologna and in Reggio nell'Emilia. Perez and Zorilla dropped out of sight. Rick flew back to Brazil. Manera left the country. Riccardo disappeared. The gang's activities continued, however. That was the beauty of this operation; the crooks could work wherever they hung their hats and put down their suitcases. Even while police units under the direction of Interpol Rome were spreading their dragnets in Italy, swindle teams were at work in New York and Zürich.

Meanwhile, in Rome, systematic police investigation came up with a lead on a white Jaguar that Cocucci had bought for Jannette. It was traced to an auto agency, whose records showed that registration documents in the name of Maria Lucia Soarez had been mailed to General Delivery, Milan, at the owner's request. The salesman was shown photographs picked up in the Via Acaia raid and pointed out his two customers, Jannette and Cocucci.

On Tuesday, April 27, the Milan police reported to Interpol Rome that at 6 P.M. that evening they had taken into custody a woman answering to the description of Maria Lucia Soarez and a white Jaguar with the license plate number listed on the registration papers. With their suspect was a baby and an elderly woman, the baby's grandmother. They also located the Milan workshop and, search warrant in hand, found that Jannette's apartment contained quantities of passports, bank checks, ID cards, driver's licenses—all the items on the now familiar inventory.

Jannette, hysterical, was hospitalized and then transferred

to Rome by ambulance. The baby and the grandmother went along with her. Cocucci, who was in Rome when the police raided his Milan apartment and workshop, transferred his home base to Bologna and moved in with Graziotti and Elena. Activity, though curtailed, continued, and so did the police investigations. Milan units of the Squadra Mobile traced gang members to Bologna, where they picked up several second- and third-echelon members, including Morinigo and Juarez. They also located the Bologna workshop and the one at Reggio nell'Emilia. The machinery and supplies confiscated in all these raids were warehoused in Milan under the control of judicial authorities.

The Bologna address used by Graziotti as living quarters was staked out. On the night of May 18 the police picked up Graziotti and Elena. With them was a priest, who was also taken into custody. The man inside the clerical garb turned out to be Cocucci.

It looked as though Interpol's war against the South American Gang was over. Through those photographs from the Via Acaia workshop, the police were able to penetrate the anonymity of gang members and leaders. Multiple names were sorted out, and people were identified by their roles in the organization. The Group D chart came to life. Police reports from the various countries could now be fully coordinated and a picture of the gang's structure and operations sketched in. Graziotti was engineer and production chief; Cocucci was the general manager of overseas operations; Manera was the specialist team leader; Rick was executive officer for the transatlantic operation. Dick Szuman in Brazil seemed to be the chief. That meant that the headquarters might be in the São Paolo area, where Dick Szuman was living openly as a businessman and the proprietor of a hotel. He was watched, but it soon became evident that the head of the conspiracy had not yet been discovered.

Meanwhile, police announced that the gang was smashed;

the workshops in four Italian cities were shut down; the equipment and supplies had been confiscated; and the members were being arrested. And the swindles continued.

In June of the same year, 1965, a team of three hit banks in a number of Caribbean islands. In September a team of five came through the islands again and went on into Miami and New York where, as we have seen, the male team members were stopped. Showers of counterfeit bank checks continued to fall periodically, now in southern Europe, now in the United States, now in northern Europe. The United States was the weak link in the potential chain of defense that Interpol was trying to construct. An example is the reaction to a crime that had occurred a year before and several thousand miles away to the south.

On October 1, 1964, Pan American Airways Flight 81 had lifted off the runway at Miami International Airport, destined for Buenos Aires. In its baggage compartment was a sealed mail pouch holding twenty-nine registered letters. Two of them contained more than 2,000 Bank of America traveler's checks worth $50,100. The checks had been registered and mailed in San Francisco three days earlier by the Bank of America to a bank in Asunción, Paraguay. Normally the packages would have been forwarded to Asunción from Buenos Aires, but when PAA 81 arrived in Buenos Aires, the pouch containing them was not unloaded with the other mail. The Argentine Postal Administration reported the pouch as "not received." A few days later, the pouch reappeared on board PAA 204 flying from Buenos Aires to Asunción. Paraguayan postal records showed receipt of the pouch, but the Bank of America packets were missing.

In the weeks that followed, nearly all the traveler's checks from those packets were cashed in banks and shops in Central America, Mexico, and France—all but seventeen of them by "persons unknown." The bank, strangely, accepted the matter calmly. It did not seek a police investigation, nor did it file an indemnity claim for its loss. For that matter, no serious attempt was made to trace the cashed checks, which, after all, might have provided nearly 2,000 clues to the perpetrators of the crime. In fact, the crime might have disappeared completely into the victimized bank's archives were it not for routine reports on missing mail that are made within the United States Postal Service. The report on this theft was routed to the desk of a United States postal inspector named Sam Flanner, who had been building up a special file on thefts of that kind. That was in 1964.

About a year later, when Manera and his two accomplices were arrested in New York on check swindling charges, three Bank of America traveler's checks were found in Manera's suitcase. Flanner, who, along with other federal agents, had been notified about the arrest, fixed his eye on those three slips of paper. From their serial numbers he was able to identify them as part of the batch stolen the previous year from the Pan American flight. These were the last three, $90 worth. All the others, $50,010 worth, had been cashed.

Flanner asked where checks had been cashed most recently and learned that fourteen of them had been cashed in New York during the ten days preceding the arrest of the Latin trio. At his request, Bank of America sent him the fourteen checks, and Flanner went to visit each shop at which checks had been cashed. He drew only blanks until he walked into Fulton-Nassau Jewels, Inc., on the Avenue of the Americas. The proprietor, Rose Glantz, recalled the customer—"a typical South American businessman." He had bought a ring for $110 and paid for it with three $50 traveler's checks. She had given him $40 in change. She had a sales record with his name, Pedro Sani; he had shown her a Paraguayan passport for identification.

Among the passports found in the luggage of Geneyro, alias Manera, alias Bisiani, was a Paraguayan passport in the name of Pedro Sani. The photograph on it was that of Manera. Ten more traveler's checks cashed in New York shops also carried the name Pedro Sani. Now the entire batch of 2,000 was sent to the Post Office Department's laboratory for examination of the fingerprints found on them. It was found that Manera had cashed about one-third of them, using a variety of names, on both sides of the Atlantic.

In March, 1966, forty counterfeit bank checks were mailed from Rome and Milan, ostensibly payable by the Banco Commerciale Italiana in favor of fraudulent accounts opened at banks in Spain, the Netherlands, Switzerland, Denmark, and Sweden. A team circled through Madrid, Barcelona, Bilbao, Geneva, Lausanne, and Copenhagen, making withdrawals of cash from those banks. The fraud attempt was discovered, and police and Banco Commercile officers issued an alert. Banks and police in other cities were standing by to nab the culprits. But the gang heard about the alert, and a telegram in code went from Rome to Copenhagen: "Mother is sick come home at once." The "tour" was immediately abandoned, but not before cash had been withdrawn on twenty-five of the forty fake bank transfer orders.

In June a million deutschmarks' worth of counterfeit bank checks were run through the banks of Germany, this time with no obstacles. Ultimately even American banks began to catch on. In March of 1967 ten banks in New York were the object of a $160,000 swindle; only $90,000 was withdrawn from six of the banks. Because the other four were alert, $70,000 worth of forgeries was not realized.

Members of the gang still are caught from time to time. Interpol's Group D and other police organizations that specialize in bank swindles are convinced that this kind of crime can be controlled. A high degree of international cooperation and coordination among banks and police agencies is required along with complete and effective use of Interpol machinery. Interpol has one of the keys to breaking such conspiracies.

The New York Five incident is a perfect example of the need for cooperation. A clue to the identity of the mastermind of the South American Gang was in the hands of a half-dozen United States agencies, investigators who might have coordinated with South American police but did not do so. Three men were arrested; their two women accomplices were released without anyone in New York knowing who they were, where they came from, or what they were doing. One of them, Ingeborg Skoruppa, could easily have been identified through European police files as the woman Manera had picked up in Germany in 1963. The other woman required a more sophisticated identification. In New York she carried a passport that said she was Maria Ipanien Taschian, a native of Uruguay, and she got away. Five months later she was arrested in Madrid, and her luck ran out. Spanish police and their Interpol bureau not only discovered her identity but also brought the core of the South American Gang one step closer to final exposure. Her passport identified her as Teresa Botti. As in New York, the crime that brought her to the attention of the police in Madrid was a check swindle at a jewelry store. Her partner was an Argentinian.

His name was Juan Carlos D'Angelo Zuliani, and he had started his criminal activities while he was still a student. Eventually, in Montevideo in 1965, he made contact with a man named Bruno Briganzi and shortly thereafter joined a group whose members were regularly furnished with fraudulent bank checks, usually drawn against American banks for sums ranging from hundreds to many thousands of dollars. In December, 1965, he was assigned to a team with two women to go on a check-cashing expedition in Brazil. One of these women used the name Teresa Botti. She had just returned to Montevideo from a similar jaunt to New York. Immediately after their return to Brazil, Teresa and Zuliani were assigned to a swing through a dozen or more European cities. They were picked up by the police in Madrid.

The Spanish police investigated and discovered that Teresa was Teresa Federici, a native of the Italian province of Cremona. At the time of her arrest she was in her late forties. She had been, according to police, mistress to a top racketeer and then to an Argentine executive and government figure, and eventually had become engaged in check-passing and bank-swindling in Montevideo. In June, 1965, an Austrian police report stated that a Teresa Federici, a Peter Wichers, and an Emilio Matera had cashed stolen and fraudulent checks in the islands of the West Indies from Aruba to Jamaica. The name Emilio Matera is pretty close to Emilio Manera; Peter Wichers was the name used by Wissocq-Bo when he opened a First National City Bank account in New York and cashed fraudulent checks in October of that same year. The Spanish police discovered that Teresa Federici alias Botti had been assigned to a team swindling New York banks in October, an expedition that had ended with Manera and Wissocq-Bo being arrested along with the third man in their party, Barcello Garcia. She then had returned to Montevideo and shipped out again with Zuliani.

Here's how Interpol Madrid put the picture together: Zuliani, a crook from a good family with connections in the social, business, and political communities of Argentina, had gravitated to a gang directed by one Briganzi. Teresa, who had connections in the upper echelons of crime in Argentina, also had gravitated to a gang directed by Briganzi. After the group—supposed to have been directed by the Szuman brothers in Italy—was busted, check-passing and bank-swindling teams directed by Briganzi continued to operate in the Western Hemisphere and in Europe.

Interpol Madrid learned from Interpol Montevideo that their records showed that a Briganzi had been the proprietor of a bar in Montevideo and that he was believed to be the head of a smuggling organization "on a grand scale," but with most of the revenue coming from the cashing of bank checks and traveler's checks, counterfeit and stolen. Montevideo police records also noted his immunity from prosecution. References to the basis for this immunity were veiled, but they could be interpreted in terms of political influence and police corruption.

In due course a report from Interpol Madrid reached Interpol headquarters in Saint-Cloud, and at Group D a new marker went up on the chart, at the top, as the staff began to assemble information to determine whether here at last was the mastermind.

To make a dent in this form of crime, to put an end to the growth of bank swindling, the banks themselves will have to establish a system of defense using at least the techniques already known. It would not be unreasonable to require bank managements to install safeguards that are at least as contemporary as their buildings and interior decoration. When Manera, Wissocq-Bo, and Garcia were put out of action, American banks may have been saved several hundreds of thousands of dollars that year, perhaps a million or two, as estimated by *The American Banker*, but the hazard was not eliminated. Banks continued to be victimized by predators with other names using approximately the same system.

These are only a few criminals among a large community that are occupied in crime of an inevitably fascinating kind. Since they work without violence, the public tends not to be outraged; since the total they take in is relatively small compared with the gross assets of the banking industry, bankers tend to be tolerant. Since the amount in absolute terms is enormous, criminal activity enjoys the large economic resources it needs for survival and growth.

By late 1966 the situation concerning the gang was as follows. Interpol Brasília reported that Dick Szuman was living off the coast of Santos under surveillance. It took years for Manera's case to be settled, but settled it was. After imprisonment and a fine, he was deported to Italy despite his attempts to avoid it.

Wissocq-Bo, a wanted man in several countries, was sent to Argentina. He was put on a nonstop airliner to Buenos Aires, and he disappeared. One explanation was that the message from New York announcing the date of his arrival and the flight was somehow undelivered, delayed, or diverted. Another guess was that this expert in false identities and phony passports somehow acquired or retained one of them and on arrival blandly walked through the Buenos Aires checkpoint.

Garcia was not so lucky. After being sentenced in New York, he was shipped to Miami to answer a fraudulent check-passing charge, and after serving his time was sent to Spain. Police were on hand to take him into custody when he arrived at the Madrid airport.

Jannette Polanski and Osvaldo Cocucci were flushed from hiding and brought to the bar of Italian justice. She lost her looks, he dropped her, and she informed. Her story in capsule is told in Interpol's portrait parle; photographs taken in the early 1960s show a face of exquisite beauty; recent photographs show the face lined and worn. The dossier has a new entry: "on drugs."

Only estimates are available of the amount of money that is annually siphoned out of banks by international swindlers. In relative terms, it is undoubtedly secondary to the banking community's total contribution to the financial sustenance of the world's criminal sub-society, but even that secondary amount is, for the criminals, a comfortably big bite. At a recent conference of bankers in Cleveland, Ohio, it was reported that United States banks lose money at the rate of $400 million annually through bad checks and related forms of check fraud. Some experts put the total higher, but all agree that the amount is far greater than the total loot pulled out by such crooks as bank robbers and burglars. At the $400 million estimate, the proceeds of check frauds would be enough to provide 20,000 fraud practitioners with annual incomes of $20,000 each. Tax-free, of course.

8
Interpol
and Counterfeiting

In June, 1968, a South African citizen, his British woman companion, and two children were traveling as a family by boat from Montevideo across the Rio de la Plata to Buenos Aires. In addition to their luggage they had a baby carriage, which they pushed ahead of them as they came off the gangplank and stopped for immigration and customs formalities. For some reason, whether because of a hunch or an informer's tip or just by chance, the customs inspector poked around in the baby carriage and found bundles of counterfeit United States currency. After the couple was arrested, the inspector and his colleagues counted 33,775 bank notes that represented 3,377,500 American dollars in bogus cash.

What makes this item of crime worth noticing is not only the ploy that the couple used and the amount of cash involved but also the perpetrators and the location. The investigation that followed the couple's arrest uncovered a counterfeit ring

141

run by two South Africans and two Englishmen. One of the South Africans was the mastermind, one of the Englishmen was the printer, and a printshop in London was their headquarters. Argentinian and South African police and Scotland Yard worked together on the case, coordinating their moves through Interpol. The principals were arrested, and the printshop, when raided, yielded another $400,000 worth of bogus money ready for circulation, along with plates, paper, and counterfeiting equipment.

Counterfeiting is a curious crime, and the public attitude toward it has been strange. During the last ten years counterfeiting has grown enormously in the United States and around the world. In America there was an increase of 700 percent or more during the decade of the 1960s, yet a major study of crime by the President's Commission on Law Enforcement and Administration of Justice of 1965–67 never mentioned it at all, nor did it explain the ommission. Counterfeiting is one of America's oldest crimes and might very well have been brought to this country by the Pilgrim fathers. At one point it threatened to wreck the federal government's effort to preserve the republic during the Civil War. In that recent multimillion-dollar Buenos Aires case, the idea of using a family group with a baby carriage as camouflage seems reminiscent of the days when counterfeiting was practiced by criminals of great cunning who matched wits with equally adroit detectives. Usually, however, counterfeiting is a most prosaic form of crime whose potential for harming society is understood by very few people.

The international attitude toward counterfeiting is unique in two ways. It was the first kind of crime against which nations banded together in an attempt to institute a "one-world" concept of criminal justice. By the Geneva Convention on Currency Counterfeiting of 1929, signatory countries in effect declared that they were one community in the suppression of counterfeiting; each country pledged to impose the same punishment on the offenders they caught regardless of whose currency was being dishonored. In other words, France was to treat an offender trafficking in bogus German bank notes as if they were French bank notes and vice versa; by law, the United States protects the currencies of all other nations equally with the American dollar, and other nations are pledged to do the same.

The uniqueness of counterfeiting also lies in the fact that it gave the fledgling Interpol an opportunity for instant recognition as an established institution. The self-generated policemen's association acquired attributes of international legal status when the League of Nations assigned to it exclusive responsibility for carrying out the league's agreement on the subject. The League of Nations' enactment remains in effect today, although the league itself no longer exists; and while only fifty-one nations are signatories (the United States being among the nonsigners at this writing), under Interpol's administration of the terms of the pact most countries do participate whether or not they themselves have joined the organization.

The attempt to attain international uniformity of criminal justice for counterfeiters is interesting because the laws regarding this crime vary so greatly among nations and also because civilized man has always been at odds with himself over how to deal with such offenders. Americans are often criticized as money-worshipers. In other cultures, however, offenses against the coin of the realm have been regarded much more severely, almost like treason. In Athens in the sixth century B.C., for instance, the punishment for counterfeiters was death. In Rome under Emperor Constantine they were burned alive, and in pre-Roman England they had their hands chopped off. During the Middle Ages counterfeiters were drawn and hung. In the days before paper money existed, a widespread method of cheating in a business deal or in paying off a debt was by clipping gold coins, snipping bits off the edges. In a parody of the dictum of the Hammurabi Code "an eye for an eye, a tooth for a tooth," some princes anticipated the more recent notion of setting the punishment to fit the crime. Coin-clippers were likely to be punished by being "clipped" themselves—losing an ear, a nose, a finger, or worse —the Normans punished counterfeiting with castration.

Today a wide variation continues: for an identical offense the counterfeiter in France might draw a sentence of life imprisonment; in the United Arab Republic, life imprisonment at hard labor; in Algeria, death; in the United States, only ten to fifteen years in a federal penitentiary.

Severity of punishment, however, does not by itself cause counterfeiting to subside. The United States Secret Service had more than 10,000 cases to handle in 1962, more than 22,000 in 1970, and, based on trends, a projected 26,000 cases in 1972. Meanwhile, free-lance money printers are known to have increased production to a rate of $27 million worth a year by the end of 1970. Production as well as distribution has been accelerating both at home and abroad, feeding the international streams of bogus money of all nations, which is increased even more by the rising tide of trade and tourism.

The idea of international joint police action against counterfeiting is relatively new in world affairs, considering that counterfeiting began more than 2,500 years ago. Effective joint efforts date from the late 1920s, when Interpol came into its own, and they have continued to evolve.

In the aftermath of World War I many new nations were formed; many European governments were struggling with complex economic problems; and the printing presses of all nations were rolling merrily along. Many countries were profligate in their production of bank notes, and many free-lance producers took advantage. Even among honest people it was not easy to tell the real from the fake. This era was made to order for thieves of all nations, especially for counterfeiters. It became a time of grandiose schemes, some in comic-opera style.

In Germany, for example, where printing press money by government fiat was rampant, the right-wing German Nationalist Party hired as a "currency consultant" a Russian refugee named Arthur Schultze, an ardent socialist who had fled the Russian Revolution. Schultze had been an engraver in the state printing works of Imperial Russia. When he left home, he carried with him a set of plates, presumably for making personal batches of Russian bank notes.

The idea of passing even genuine Czarist paper money after the revolution, let alone counterfeit money, may seem as unlikely a prospect as passing Confederate ten-dollar bills in Macy's. However, Germany of the early 1920s was flooded with printing press money in such quantities that Schultze's paper seemed no worse than any other. The Versailles Treaty had saddled Germany with reparations to the tune of $33 billion, and certain patriotic Germans were trying to figure out a way for the fatherland to evade the burden. General Erich von Ludendorff and a few kindred spirits had gone into politics and were busy concocting such schemes when they heard about Arthur Schultze. They seized upon the idea of having him manufacture a quantity of French 1,000-franc bank notes that would be used for reparations payments to the Allies. But the scheme fell apart very quickly.

Schultze then was taken in hand by a Hungarian prince named Windischgraetz, whose ideas were even more visionary. The prince assembled a glittering coterie of nobles, military officers, academicians, and technicians to launch a plot that included the printing of $100 million worth of French 1,000-franc notes. They meant to use these to recoup their own depressed fortunes and at the same time to wreck the economy of their victorious enemy, France. They also hoped to finance a seizure of the Hungarian government and to restore Hungary's imperial heir to the throne.

Schultze was hired as a technician and was promised handsome compensation. The scheme was elaborately conceived but clumsily executed. A time schedule had been arranged for disposal of the bogus money all at once by couriers in several foreign cities. One of the insiders thought he would pass a bit for his own account ahead of the schedule. The premature appearance of the counterfeit bills alerted police, who then were ready and waiting when the couriers went to their tasks on schedule. One after another, the conspirators were apprehended, tried, and convicted. The plot to seize the Hungarian government fared no better. Schultze was sent to prison with the others and died in his cell under mysterious circumstances suggesting that he may have been murdered to prevent him from turning state's evidence.

Such conspiracies by amateur crooks were only the sideshow. The professional criminals who came back into circulation after World War I found the new countries with their economic dislocations especially vulnerable to the crafts of bogus money. Interpol's involvement in counterfeiting began during this period.

The director of Viennese police in 1923 had taken historic action on two fronts. To strike back at the counterfeiters on a mutual-aid basis with his colleagues in other countries he launched a publication, the *Counterfeits and Forgeries Review*. It was to serve as an informational clearinghouse on bogus money produced and circulated in Europe. His other action was to call the international conference of police officials that resulted in the formation of what is today known as Interpol.

Meanwhile, the governments of several European nations that were fearful of being inundated by the rising tide of bogus money insisted on bringing the problem before the League of Nations. In 1926 a committee was named to study the matter. It formulated three principles: (1) there would have to be a permanent basis of international action; (2) national laws against counterfeiting would have to be standardized; and (3) police work of all nations in this field would have to be centralized and coordinated.

These ideas were crystallized in the 1929 Geneva Convention on Currency Counterfeiting, which was signed at the time by representatives of twenty-six nations. Thus groundwork was laid for dealing with counterfeiting as an international problem more than forty years ago; translating it into effective action was something else again.

The Geneva Convention sets forth certain of the basics—a commonly accepted definition of the crime of counterfeiting and standards for the administration of criminal justice against offenders, for the conduct of investigations, and for the interchange of information by investigative bodies. It became a practical exercise in international law enforcement, except for one thing—the question of carrying out the ideas.

The League of Nations had no machinery for carrying out the provisions of its Geneva Convention. Interpol, however, did. In 1931 an International Counterfeiting Conference was held. It was agreed that the international police organization should take over. Interpol also assumed responsibility for publishing the *Counterfeits and Forgeries Review*. This has become a unique reference guide to bogus currencies of the world.

A second International Counterfeiting Conference was organized under Interpol's leadership in June, 1935, in Copenhagen. The conference emphasized improved reporting on counterfeiting cases so that Interpol could more effectively act as a central information office for this crime. The original Geneva Convention had recognized the importance of tracking counterfeiters from country to country. One of its basic provisions was that when an offender was caught his criminal record in other countries should be obtained so that the courts could charge him and penalize him as a habitual offender even if his crime was his first offense in the last country to catch him. The conference reemphasized this. It was to increase Interpol's importance and responsibility as an international crime-fighting agency in the period between the two world wars.

Like World War I, World War II brought forth a number

of new nations, each producing its share of new bank notes—both genuine and counterfeit—to add to the world's supply.

Interpol resumed its mandated International Currency Conferences after World War II, at The Hague in 1950, in Copenhagen in 1961, and in Mexico City in 1969. Meanwhile Interpol continued to develop facilities for technical expertise in detection, in its laboratory work, and in its reference files of both genuine and bogus bank notes. It established a section in the International Criminal Police Coordination Division, Group F, devoted entirely to counterfeiting. Among other specialties, it has staff experts who are qualified as witnesses for testifying in court when cases are tried. Use of experts is sometimes more effective than attempting to get someone to travel from the country whose currency has been imitated. Some countries, in fact, do not print their own currency but contract it out to private printing establishments; therefore the nation itself may have no official who is able to qualify as an expert.

Today several new wrinkles have developed in the practice of the art of counterfeiting, not the least of which is the increasing number of counterfeiters. In the United States the annual production of counterfeit bills went from less than a half-million dollars' worth in 1960 to $19 million worth in 1970. In terms of printing activity, this represented an increase of from less than 18,000 printed pieces a year to about one and one-quarter million pieces in those years. The trend seems to be steadily upward; in 1972 the Secret Service said it was detecting counterfeits at the rate of $25 million worth a year.

Between $3 million and $5 million in counterfeit American currency is estimated as circulating annually outside the United States. Add to this the production abroad of 260 million Italian lire, over 5 million Spanish pesetas, a million West African francs, a half-million Canadian dollars, and so on (these figures are reported levels in 1968), and it becomes strikingly evident that the presses are rolling at a record rate around the world.

The professionals tend to operate on a mass production basis. A single plant discovered in Switzerland in 1971 yielded seizures of over $4 million of fake United States bank notes. How much bogus currency is actually passed on to the public, however, is not known precisely. For reasons explained later, more is printed than passed. Interpol has been asked to assemble statistics on quantities passed each year.

Much of this counterfeiting is aimed at the tourist trade. With an estimated 50 million persons a year traveling outside their own countries and needing to convert their money to that of the countries they are visiting, the exchange of national currencies reaches large proportions. Amidst these hundreds of thousands of daily foreign exchange transactions in every corner of the globe the opportunities for sharp practices are bound to attract criminals. Exchanging one's familiar currency for strange foreign money has become a widespread hazard, especially among tourists who can be drawn into a "better rate of exchange" by sidewalk moneychangers and street-corner tipsters. Travelers provide counterfeiters with one basic market. Another is the narcotics traffic, since traditionally these two kinds of criminality often function in tandem.

Interpol's role in the fight against counterfeiting is technical and strategic while its everyday work in this field is peculiarly its own. For example, in 1968 a Greek was arrested in Germany for passing fifty-pound British bank notes. Interpol had previously issued a wanted notice on him for fraud in Switzerland on the basis of which he had been previously arrested in Germany and extradited to Swiss authorities to stand trial. When arrested for the second time in Germany, he was readily identified, his entire criminal career was exposed through Interpol files, and he was jailed.

High mobility is an ordinary feature of the counterfeit traffic, and this factor alone complicates all efforts at its control. Two Italians were convicted recently in Germany after passing American twenty-dollar bills in several German cities.

When Interpol circulated information on them, Swiss police identified them as having passed similar counterfeits in their country during the previous year. Investigation further disclosed that another member of their group was operating out of Pisa, Italy, and that he belonged to a gang based in Sardinia.

The country most affected has been the United States. A side effect of its affluence and economic expansion has been its emergence as the prime target for the world's bogus money conspirators. Yet the American public, like people everywhere, seems to show no special concern except for sensational "cops and robbers" stories in the press. Here, too, there has been a radical change in what is required for holding public attention. Not long ago the disclosure of a few hundred thousand dollars' worth of bogus money was given front-page newspaper treatment. In 1969 a case in which the United States Secret Service seized $4,400,000 worth of counterfeits in California rated exactly four sentences in an Associated Press wire service story. Formerly one of the more glamorous crimes, counterfeiting today tends to be regarded as prosaic.

During the 1960s United States government agents were increasingly successful at breaking up counterfeiting rings and seemed to be getting ahead. Agents' annual seizures of finished bogus bank notes before circulation increased from about $190,000 in fiscal 1960 to over $16 million in fiscal 1970. The growing international focus of counterfeiting, however, showed a picture with new dimensions and made Interpol more important than ever. Even if the Secret Service ever does get the domestic scene completely in hand, there will still be a problem in bogus American currency produced abroad for foreign distribution around the world. In 1971 at least 58 new issues of bogus American dollars came out of foreign plants and 256 from domestic. In actuality no expert sees either the domestic or foreign traffic in counterfeit coming to an end.

By maintaining a central office for keeping track of counterfeits the world over, Interpol is able to report on the longevity of bogus money. One impressive instance had to do with a printing plant discovered to be the source of bogus twenty- and one-hundred-dollar United States bank notes in 1950. These bills had first been detected in 1948; eighteen years after the printing plant had been shut down, bank notes from that same issue were still found circulating in six countries.

As Secret Service agents continue to improve their capabilities in suppressing domestic counterfeiting, the success of criminals operating outside the country appears relatively greater. In 1966 a ring set up shop in a private home in Bergenfield, New Jersey, and operated for nearly a year without being detected, turning out million-dollar amounts of federal currency for disposal in South America. It was only when they attempted to pass bogus twenty-dollar bills in the metropolitan New York area that they got into trouble; within a few days they were detected and rounded up, and their plant was seized.

The production and passing of counterfeit United States currency in foreign lands has grown at a faster rate than domestic production. The $5 million worth of counterfeit American bank notes known to have been printed abroad in 1968 was almost a third of the amount printed in this country during the same year. Foreign output in 1968 was more than one and one-half times the amount actually detected within the United States during 1965, only three years earlier.

South America, target of the Bergenfield counterfeiters, is only one vulnerable area. During 1968 fake United States currency was found circulating in forty-two countries around the world, from Algeria and Australia to Yemen and Yugoslavia, including eight African countries. But while the American dollar has greatest popularity among counterfeit traffickers, it is not the only currency that interests them. Over fifty nations have had new counterfeit issues of their currency put into circulation over the last ten years, in about 200 issues. Many of them circulated in only one or two countries outside their own national borders, but bogus French francs passed in three foreign countries, British and Canadian currency in five, and Italian in six. It is estimated that, of the hundreds of issues of counterfeits of all nations that appeared around the world during the 1960s, less than two dozen circulated exclusively within their own national boundaries. Altogether almost 1,500 different counterfeit issues of the currencies of all nations have been circulated internationally during the last decade.

American experience with foreign counterfeiting goes back at least to the turn of the century. An early instance dates back to 1900, when bogus five-dollar bills were being produced in Italy and smuggled into New York packed in olive oil cans by a notorious American gangster named Morello. Morello got away with it for a couple of years. When he decided to transfer production to an upper New York State location, however, he was promptly caught.

Moving with the times, European counterfeiters have attempted to pass their product in the United States. Shortly after World War II a group headquartered in Marseille devised a novel method for passing about $2 million worth of phony bills in hundreds, fifties, and twenties. They saw an opportunity in the stream of displaced persons who were then emigrating to the United States. They exchanged their counterfeit United States currency for the emigrants' good European money and for jewelry or other valuables. The quality of these counterfeits was good, and they were not detected for five months. About $60,000 worth was passed by the unsuspecting victims before the alert went out. Three Secret Service agents were sent to France, where Franco-American military cooperation was still in effect and where the American officers were able to obtain the direct assistance of French police. They trailed the ring from Paris to Marseille and located the gang's workshops in a private house and a hunting lodge about twenty miles outside the city. Raids and arrests by the French police put an end to that enterprise.

During the 1960s it became obvious that counterfeits were being produced regularly in foreign printshops from Australia and Hong Kong to England and Italy. American law enforcement began to move in the direction indicated. In 1963 the United States Secret Service established an office in Paris as a base for investigations in Europe, the Near East, and Africa. This gave the agency direct contact with Interpol and with the police of all those areas. Since then the Secret Service has established offshore offices in Honolulu for the Far East and in San Juan for South America.

Interpol experts classify three basic kinds of persons who engage in counterfeiting—the printing house employee who surreptitiously uses his employer's facilities for clandestine production on his own account, the printer who decides that since he has the facilities he might as well use them, and the professional criminal who is entrenched in the criminal subsociety of his area and functions as an entrepreneur.

The third kind is the most dangerous and is to be found in all parts of the world, according to Interpol reports. This kind organizes the activity so that specific tasks are assigned to individuals in production, transportation, accounting, and wholesale and retail distribution. This enterprise is usually only one of several in which the top man is engaged, drug trafficking and smuggling being the most frequent lines. He keeps himself safe from lawmen by insulating himself from the actual operation through the employment of intermediaries. He is also likely to have numerous contacts in other sectors of the criminal community, and through them he explores international opportunities for distribution.

Early in 1969 Interpol Washington learned of five Lebanese persons who were arrested in Beirut with $1,850 worth of United States counterfeit currency in their possession. They had received it from one of their countrymen in Vienna. Following a routine inquiry to the Austrian bureau on the Interpol network, Viennese police arrested a sixth Lebanese with evidence that he was trafficking in narcotics.

These six, however, were only lower-echelon members of the ring.

The interlocking of counterfeiting with drug traffic seems to be one of the basic international patterns charted by Interpol. Later in 1969 Spanish police stopped and interrogated a Spaniard going through the customs checkpoint at Ceuta. They found him carrying bogus German deutschmarks, which he admitted having received in Morocco. By exchanging information on the Interpol network, Spanish and Moroccan police traced a German ring that had set up shop in Morocco for putting deutschmarks into circulation. The Spanish courier arrested at Ceuta was found to be in the drug traffic; he had received bogus deutschmarks in exchange for a delivery of hashish.

In recent years entrepreneurial criminal types have introduced yet other factors into the picture—the principles and techniques of business management. They operate not on a shoestring but backed with adequate financing. The typical counterfeit mastermind is likely to "play percentages," expecting successful distribution of only a part of his output; therefore, he is likely to set up a huge production, expecting the cops sooner or later to make seizures—by which time his organization, he hopes, will have passed a profitable amount. The seizures are not a loss but simply another cost of doing business.

The experience of William Lee Stanley illustrates this practice. He organized a professional enterprise with Isaiah Adam Cain during the summer of 1968. For the next year and a half they operated successively out of five locations, moving along as each one became hazardous or was raided, their counterfeits seized, their employees arrested. During their period of operation, however, they passed some $420,000 worth of bogus money. Stanley, the ringleader, had his case dismissed after the gang was apprehended.

The "planned loss" approach seems similar to practices in legitimate business. Many merchants, manufacturers, and banks write off losses due to shoplifting, employee pilferage, and embezzlement or check fraud as part of the expense of doing business.

For this reason, what Interpol describes as the entrepreneurial type of counterfeiter seems to have had a major effect in ballooning this class of world crime. The quantity of counterfeit currency successfully passed in the United States increased from less than a quarter of a million dollars' worth in fiscal 1961 to almost $3 million worth in fiscal 1969. During this period, while the seizures of counterfeit money by government agents increased impressively, the dollar amount of the money that was passed grew sixfold.

These developments suggest that counterfeiting has acquired dimensions that more than justify Interpol's early concern with it as a special area of criminality. To cite one measure of growth, more than 870 kinds of counterfeit currency of all nations were issued during the 1950s; during the 1960s, there were 1,500 new kinds.

Since workshops for counterfeiting seem to spring up everywhere, the search for them has become a regular item on many police agendas, with Interpol channeling information for tracking bogus money back to its sources. During a single twelve-month period early in the 1970s, such workshops were being uncovered in Brazil, South Africa, Germany, Belgium, Guatemala, India, Indonesia, Pakistan, England, and Switzerland as well as in the United States.

Gangs engaged in bogus money traffic now have multinational membership as well as dealing in multiple criminal activities. In 1968, for instance, German police arrested a German man and woman for passing Spanish bank notes that had been manufactured in Düsseldorf. The arrest led to a raid and roundup of a gang headquartered in Barcelona. The gang consisted of a number of Greeks, a Dutchman, and a Spaniard besides the two Germans. They all were engaged in simultaneous traffic in drugs and women as well as counterfeit cash.

Bogus American money is the most international of all fake

cash. The London-South Africa group whose case opened this chapter actually functioned without any Americans involved, even though they were trafficking in American counterfcits. In 1968 Interpol facilities became essential to police of three nations after Australian currency was detected circulating in Germany. When the German police began to trace it through Interpol, they found that it had originated in Australia with a ring that included one American and six Australians. When the printshop was raided by Australian police it was turning out American bank notes. The American member had been convicted previously of counterfeiting and forgery in his native land.

Even within the continental United States big cases have come to light in recent years involving rings of offshore origin. The principals of a Cuban-Latin American gang detected and apprehended in March, 1969, were named Gonzales, Castenero, Pino, and Castro. The year before, a New Jersey-based group captured with a stockpile of more than $3 million in counterfeit twenty-dollar bills included people with names like Dixon, DeSalvo, Horsley, Ciccia, Bisulea, and Santoro.

The indications of what lies ahead in the world of counterfeiting foretell more than internationalization and modernization of operating methods. Its shadow touches financial instruments of even larger importance, such as checks, securities, and credit cards. Counterfeiters, traditionally involved mainly with bank notes, have turned their attention in this direction for the opportunity it offers.

The volume of privately issued forms of financial value pouring through the channels of commerce has reached flood proportions. In the United States alone at the start of the 1970s, for example, an estimated 3 to 4 million merchants, hotels, and other businesses were regularly accepting payment through credit cards from over 35 million customers. The expansion of tourism, the fast-growing credit-card economy, the international transfers of deposits and investments involve not only huge and growing sums, but also a vast circulation of these plastic instruments of monetary exchange reaching all parts of the globe. Interpol has been watching this situation for years, but mainly as an observer.

It is standard practice in the criminal justice systems of most nations to treat offenders against private financial instruments such as traveler's checks, credit cards, money orders, stocks, and bonds with greater leniency than offenders against legal currency and government bonds. In line with this practice, police investigations of offenses against private financial paper are conducted on a lower key. But this traditional approach has ominous implications because of the amounts now involved. In currency crimes the units are relatively small —five-, ten-, fifty-, and one-hundred-dollar denominations and their foreign currency equivalents. In credit card counterfeiting the amounts can run up to tens of thousands of dollars. Stock certificates and bonds are issued in thousand- and million-dollar units.

The state of the art for bogus production is very significant on this point. According to a statement from American Bank Note Company, "Today's counterfeiter has at his disposal the equipment and ability to produce reasonably deceptive simulations of stock certificates or bonds." Even more significant, a sophisticated and subtle technique is evolving by which bogus industrial securities are channeled into the complex world of banking and corporate finance, domestic and international.

In its most generally successful form, this kind of scheme uses counterfeit shares or counterfeit corporate bonds as collateral to obtain bank loans. In a relatively small case during 1969, a man named Seymour Franklin negotiated a $45,000 bank loan by furnishing bogus shares of Western Electric supposedly worth $75,000 to his bank as collateral. He was caught and jailed, but other instances have demonstrated that much larger frauds are commonplace and do not come to light until the certificates change hands a few times and the swindler becomes untraceable. The shares are put away in a bank's vault until the loan falls into default and the shares are sold, usually through a broker, along with other large security transactions. They then go into the frenetic channels of securities trading so that there is no particular time at which they reach the transfer agent who checks them against corporation records. By the time he determines that they are false, tracing them back to the crook is extremely difficult. Typically, a long, tedious investigation is needed to track down the origin of the bogus shares and to locate the rest of the issue. Just as typically, the victims are either not equipped or not inclined to initiate such an investigation. At one point in recent years, at least seventeen major American corporations were known to have had their share certificates counterfeited.

Meanwhile, such counterfeiting became a field in which the organized crime syndicates believed they could maneuver. Prosecutors involved in these cases have described the late 1960s as an era when organized crime "discovered Wall Street." At first the interest of crime syndicates was in stolen securities, but members had little experience in the mysteries of the stock exchanges and became highly vulnerable to detection. When Lenny Conforti was arrested at his home during an investigation of an extortion charge, a detective noticed a 100-share certificate of Pepsi-Cola Company stock simply lying under the suspect's bed. Checking the certificate number with the corporate stock transfer agent identified it as part of a $2,200,000 theft of securities from a prominent brokerage firm, Goodbody & Company, Inc. Until that moment the stolen shares had been passing in out-of-sight transactions, but very soon after identification of Conforti's shares investigators were able to trace and disclose the involvement of known members of the New York crime syndicates and their efforts to infiltrate the Wall Street securities brokerage industry.

Having discovered Wall Street, the criminal syndicates looked for methods of cashing more securities without trading them in places where they were likely to be matched against records of stolen ones. The primary method was to use the securities as collateral for bank loans and then, instead of being limited by the supply of stolen genuine securities, to operate the racket with illicit facsimiles.

When an issue of Indiana State Toll Road Bonds was being printed, someone had the idea of simply letting the presses run a while longer than officially scheduled. The overrun went into clandestine distribution. More commonly, a certificate is purchased legitimately and then duplicated in large quantities, not for sale but for bank loans. In a 1968 case a million-dollar loan was negotiated on collateral of Standard Oil Company stock certificates. One bank handled the arrangements on behalf of a group of banks, each making part of the loan and receiving a portion of the shares. Each bank then put its shares in its vault to hold until the loan was redeemed, none of them suspecting that the certificates were bogus.

The printing job was excellent, but the printer failed to serialize all his certificate numbers. A vault clerk in one of the smaller banks noticed that there was duplication of certificate numbers. At first he thought it was an error. He consulted the transfer agent of the stock and eventually learned that the shares he was handling, and those held by the other banks in the group loan, were counterfeit. Except for this clerk's chance observation, those stocks would have quietly rested in the banks' vaults for a long time. Prosecutors who have become familiar with this phase of crime syndicate operations believe that bank vaults all over America contain large numbers of both stolen and counterfeit securities that have not been detected by bank officers.

Although the securities industry has taken countermeasures, more sophisticated patterns of disposal have emerged, notably in overseas transactions. When sent overseas for deposit as assets or as collateral for loans, counterfeit or stolen securities become more difficult to detect, especially when anonymous European numbered bank accounts are used. Stocks and bonds handled this way can generate funds that can be transferred within Europe or elsewhere in the world or back to the United States for investment or even in moves to obtain control of corporations. Interpol has responded to this new phase by setting up its specialist Group G in the International Criminal Police Coordination Division of the Secretariat at Saint-Cloud. Group G works on general economic and financial crimes with a four-man international team of investigators. But the major thrust in foiling such frauds is with the financial institutions concerned and the control measures they must adopt.

This concern with financial instruments other than traditional money has inevitably expanded to counterfeit checks, another route for printing-press criminals to follow. The enormously expanded international use of banker's checks and traveler's checks—inevitably accompanied by easy negotiability—has attracted increasing attention from the counterfeiting fraternity. In recent years the press runs for these efforts have been very high. In a recent case, which began with the arrest of two Italian nationals in France for possession of $8,000 worth of American traveler's checks, investigations coordinated through Interpol ultimately discovered a printshop in Spain with $3 million worth of such checks ready for distribution. They were excellent imitations of those issued by a leading American bank.

Interpol has always made its facilities fully available to police investigating cases of bogus bank checks and traveler's checks. In the past, however, these were handled like other forms of fraud against private parties. Check counterfeiting was kept separate from currency counterfeiting, and in this Interpol was following both the traditional policeman's viewpoint and its specific mandate under the Geneva Convention. Strong measures and strategies were reserved to "legally authorized" monetary instruments. In the late 1960s, however, it became evident that bogus check distribution had grown too large not to be examined more thoroughly and that counterfeit currency and counterfeit traveler's checks were tending toward unification. Printshops were found turning out both or switching back and forth; criminal entrepreneurs were tending to operate with both.

Agitation began within Interpol's ranks as early as the International Currency Conference of 1950 for counterfeiting of private securities and checks to be treated similarly to currency counterfeiting. The Geneva Convention in a sense had opened the door by providing that experts from the banking field should be invited to participate in the official effort to suppress counterfeiting. The prevailing view, however, continued to be that fake instruments of financial value imitating private issues should be treated separately from official, legally authorized instruments. Police agencies feared that they would simply be swamped if they took securities and private checks under their jurisdiction. Moreover, they were familiar with an all too prevalent tendency among many businesses to hush up counterfeiters' attacks against their paper by not pushing investigations and prosecutions. Those who opposed extending the Geneva Convention also were able to point out that after more than thirty years only a minority of nations had actually signed and ratified the convention. The expansion of counterfeiting of securities and other private financial paper counterfeiting, however, continued.

At the General Assembly of 1967 in Kyoto, Japan, Interpol decided to open a large-scale inquiry into the current status of the counterfeiting of such means of payment as bank transfers, drafts, letters of credit, credit cards, and traveler's checks as well as official currency. During the discussion it was reported that traveler's check fraud had become the darling of the members of organized gangs, who would arrive in Europe together and in the space of a few days cash huge sums of traveler's checks using fake passports, which they passed around to escape identification and to evade police. It was also reported that traveler's checks and bank checks of many countries were being counterfeited, but that American dollar traveler's checks were the most popular among world criminals.

A small but basic difficulty for police emerges from the legal difference between a piece of currency and a bank check or traveler's check. The person who accepts counterfeit currency is liable under the laws of most countries to lose it through confiscation without recourse. Therefore, the public can be induced to be alert and to cooperate with authorities in suppression of counterfeits. In the case of bank checks and traveler's checks, however, it is the prerogative of the issuing bank or financial institution to decide whether the acceptor of a counterfeit will be penalized or whether the issuer will redeem the bogus check. If the issuer does redeem the fake, the acceptor loses nothing and tends to lose interest in cooperating in the suppression of the traffic. One of the large issuers of traveler's checks, Bank of America, has widely announced that it will redeem counterfeit and fraudulently cashed traveler's checks. Its object is to encourage merchants and banks to accept checks issued under its name as a way of increasing business. Losses through counterfeiting are simply accounted as a cost of doing business.

The Bank of America announcement reflects a practice that is widespread throughout American business—that of accepting many fraud and crime losses as routine. The rationale is that such losses are only a small percent of their total revenue and that to eliminate them might be troublesome or costly. The loss can be covered by insurance or absorbed among shareholders at the cost of a few pennies or dollars each. On the other hand, even a small percent of the assets of a large bank or a modern corporation can be a very large sum, capable of providing large resources for criminal subsocieties.

At the International Counterfeiting Conference called by

Interpol in Mexico City in 1969, the General Secretariat recognized the need for increased effort to protect traveler's checks and privately issued financial paper. It called for improved technology on the part of private issuers of such items, and it recommended that each nation develop its own legislation with more realistic penalties for counterfeiting stocks, bonds, bank checks, and traveler's checks. It also proposed that police in each country be given training of appropriate technical level in this field. The point seemed to be that those who professed concern should set their own house in order for effective control over this kind of crime before looking to Interpol.

Still, the international organization is steadily becoming more involved with private financial paper. It has already started collecting examples of bogus checks and securities for a central international file, and at the 1971 General Assembly the Secretariat indicated that it would start publishing a "counterfeits and forgeries review" devoted to bogus traveler's checks of all nations, similar to its famous review of counterfeit currencies of the world.

Interpol is likely to expand its work against counterfeit securities, traveler's checks, and bank checks in the years ahead; but neither the police of any one country, nor Interpol, nor social reformers, for that matter, can effectively control this area of crime until the financial community, national and international, itself develops adequate crime prevention systems, motivated by self-interest, the protection of shareholders, and a larger measure of social responsibility.

9
Interpol and Drugs

THE thirty-seventh session of Interpol's General
Assembly was held in Tehran. It opened on October 1, 1968.
The first day's meeting was rounded off with a late night
dinner given for the delegates by Lieutenant General
Mobasser, chief of the Iranian police, at the Police Officer's
Club on the slopes of Mount Elborz. The delegates were
treated to vodka lime, Caspian caviar, kebabs, meat in parsley
and lime sauces, grilled mutton and chicken served with
Iranian rice—rice mixed with chicken and lemons—and a va-
riety of exotic drinks.

The days that followed were filled with assembly sessions,
visits to police academies, concerts of Iranian folk music, and
displays by young Iranians of juggling feats that required
great strength and grace. In addition, the delegates were flown
to Isfahan for a weekend in Scheherezade country. From the
highest terrace of the Ali-Qapu Palace, Interpol members
gazed down on the mosaic domes and shining minarets of that

fabled city, visited famous mosques and other landmarks, and felt themselves carried back into the Arabian Nights. They also felt a distinct reluctance to leave Isfahan when the weekend was over.

Ahead of them lay the day-to-day problems of crime that occupied most of their waking hours. One problem in particular must have nagged at the back of many a delegate's mind, perhaps even as he was enjoying the pleasures of Isfahan. His Excellency Amir Abbas Hoveyda, the prime minister of Iran, had dropped a time bomb into the middle of the assembly's first session. In one breath he had cited "the sinister narcotic network which spans the globe . . . threatening the lives of the younger generation," and in the next he had intimated that Iran might resume cultivation of the opium poppy.

The fertile fields of Iran are capable of producing 800 to 1,320 tons of opium annually. In 1955 Iran voluntarily gave up its opium industry as an act of good will and international cooperation. By prohibiting the cultivation of poppies, it deprived its citizens of approximately $10 million in annual income—or up to three times that much if the opium crop were sold on the black market. Now, after thirteen years, Iran was considering resumption of production.

Interpol regards narcotics as the biggest problem it faces in its efforts to combat international crime. Public health authorities regard it as one of civilized man's major health hazards. A large amount of the world's narcotics supply is used legitimately for medical purposes, but a vastly greater amount is used nonmedically. Much, but not all, of this latter supply is produced, distributed, and consumed clandestinely. During the 1960s an increasing number of young people became interested in trying their hands at a bit of smuggling. By 1972 nearly a thousand young Americans were languishing in jails all over Europe, Africa, the Middle East, and Mexico. Forty-one of them, for example, were in Spanish prisons for trying to smuggle hashish from North Africa. The Spanish authorities take this sort of thing seriously, and their law calls for a mandatory minimum sentence of six years.

The smuggling of drugs, of course, has not been limited to Americans or to young people. A report published by Lebanese authorities described the arrests of Britons, Danes, New Zealanders, and Germans, among others, at ages ranging from seventeen to sixty-four.

According to Interpol, in one ten-month period during which records were kept, tourists in Europe—both students and other travelers—accounted for more than 50 percent of the marijuana, hashish, and related products seized and 28 percent of the opium. They were found transporting amounts ranging from a few grams to five or six pounds each after visits to Eastern countries.

The trend among young people is a new and disturbing feature of the world drug problem. Not long ago it was diplomats who held the spotlight. Diplomats are of special interest to master drug criminals because their luggage is immune from customs inspection. The case of Mauricio Rosal is a minor classic. Rosal, a suave and respected career diplomat from a genteel South American family, was apprehended in New York in 1964. His story, however, began with a Frenchman in Beirut in 1960. Through United States participation in Interpol and courtesy of the Lebanese police authorities, the United States Bureau of Narcotics had an agent stationed in that city. The agent, Paul Knight, received a tip concerning a French narcotics trafficker named Tarditi who was known to have been involved in morphine smuggling between Lebanon and France. The big-time criminal narcotics traffic in those days was highly compartmentalized, so when an informant passed the word that Tarditi was making trips to New York, the news received special attention.

At Knight's request the French Sûreté Nationale pinpointed

a particular trip Tarditi had made to New York, and the United States Bureau of Narcotics office in New York was instructed to find out about that trip. Checking airline manifests, they found the airline he had used and the flight he had taken. Then they studied the passenger lists. One fellow passenger, Mauricio Rosal, the Guatemalan ambassador to Belgium and Holland, attracted their attention because he had had VIP treatment from the airline. The Bureau of Narcotics began to keep a record of the movements of Tarditi and Rosal. They soon observed that Rosal made frequent trips across the Atlantic, that Tarditi made trips at about the same times, and that each time the weight of the ambassador's baggage varied by about 100 pounds on incoming and outgoing trips.

Finally Bureau agents were ready to test their inferences. On Rosal's next trip they tailed him when he arrived in New York. He claimed diplomatic immunity at the customs barrier as an ambassador in transit to his homeland, then checked into a hotel in midtown Manhattan. Tarditi was already registered there. After a couple of days in New York, Rosal canceled his onward flight to Guatemala. The Narcotics Bureau agents assumed that this canceled his diplomatic status. They continued their surveillance and saw him carrying four suitcases out of the hotel with Tarditi. The agents followed them to a meeting with two other men—a TWA airline purser named Bourbonnais and an underworld character named Calamaris. The agents then closed in, and the Guatemalan ambassador shortly thereafter became the former Guatemalan ambassador.

Interpol itself avoids involvement where ambassadors are concerned. But individual investigators working together have found that one ambassador sometimes leads to another. French police agents suspected that Rosal had been in contact with a certain Gilbert Coscia, and that put them on to the Lambro case. Lambro was a mystery man for years. His name kept turning up in cables to Marseille, the European staging point for shipments of heroin to the United States. The French police believed Gilbert Coscia to be a leading Marseille narcotics operator. They screened about 1,200,000 cables coming from the United States, Cuba, and Beirut into Marseille and noticed that a courier, Lambro, was frequently mentioned in Coscia's cables. Finally someone caught on—*Lambro* was a contraction for the French word *l'ambassadeur*. But which *ambassadeur*?

American agents and French police scrutinized airline manifests and hotel registers in New York, Paris, and Marseille, coordinated them with the cables, and found that there seemed to be a pattern—the Mexican ambassador to Bolivia, Salvator Pardo-Bolland, had taken trips to New York at the same time that Coscia was a visitor there. The simultaneous visits could have been coincidental, of course, but police in France, the United States, and Canada continued to study their movements and found that they had also made co-incidental simultaneous visits to Nice, Paris, and Montreal.

In February, 1964, something new was added. Pardo-Bolland turned up in Nice carrying a fake Uruguayan passport and was seen in conversation not only with Coscia but also with another diplomat, the Uruguayan minister-designate to the Soviet Union, Juan Arizti. It later developed that the two diplomats were old acquaintances from their former days in the Middle East.

While the police of three countries watched their itineraries and coordinated countermoves through the Interpol bureaus, Pardo-Bolland flew to Nice, Paris, and New York while Arizti flew to Nice, Paris, and Montreal. Unknown to both, Coscia's contact with the United States heroin syndicate, a Frenchman named René Buchon, had gone by ship to Baltimore and by train to New York.

Arizti left his hotel in Nice with two suitcases and arrived in Montreal with six suitcases. He was waved through customs when he showed his diplomatic passport and taxied to the Queen Elizabeth Hotel. He stopped off, however, at Central

Station, which connects with the hotel by an underground passageway, and put four of his suitcases into two rental lockers before checking into the hotel suite reserved for him.

He stayed at the Queen Elizabeth for three days, waiting for a signal and periodically checking the lockers to see that the suitcases were safe. During that time, agents of the Royal Canadian Mounted Police opened the lockers with skeleton keys, inspected his luggage, and found it loaded with 110 pounds of pure heroin in half-kilo packages. The Mounties removed the heroin and substituted identical packages containing flour, except for two packets that they left undisturbed for court evidence.

On the third day the Uruguayan reclaimed his suitcases from the lockers and took the night train to New York, where he placed four of them in lockers at Penn Station. Then he taxied to his hotel, the Elysee, where his friend Pardo-Bolland was already a guest. Immediately, Pardo-Bolland telephoned the Americana Hotel and asked to be connected with Mr. Blanc. But no Mr. Blanc was registered.

In a panic, Pardo-Bolland fired off a cable to Coscia, who was for the moment calling himself Carmen Lopez, at the Hotel Maryland, Cap d'Antibes, France. The cable read, "Cousin not located. Lorenzo." Coscia, however, was not upset; as a security measure he had arranged an initial false contact for his courier just in case he was intercepted en route.

By return wire Coscia advised that his contact in New York, René Buchon, was registered at the Americana Hotel under the name of Jacques Leroux. The diplomats promptly met "Leroux" and handed over the keys to the Penn Station locker. All three then checked out of their hotels. The diplomats booked flights out of New York. Leroux was quickly identified by the Narcotics Bureau as a notorious French narcotics smuggler and arrested on the street. Arizti and Pardo-Bolland were picked up at the airport.

Drug smuggling cases of this kind still occur from time to

time. In November, 1971, a Philippine diplomat and a Bangkok merchant were arrested in a mid-Manhattan hotel with thirty-four pounds of heroin in their suitcases. A federal agent had followed them halfway around the world before making the arrest. Nevertheless, the pattern has changed enormously.

From its headquarters in Saint-Cloud, Interpol is in a unique position to chart the international trends. Group E of the International Criminal Police Coordination Division receives and coordinates intelligence from around the world. It also maintains liaison with the United Nations Commission on Narcotic Drugs, exchanging technical information and gaining medical expertise.

In the fall of 1969 Interpol prepared an extraordinary report for the General Assembly in Mexico City that went virtually unnoticed at the time by the press and the public. It said, in effect, that events and developments in the preceding few years had "revolutionized" criminal narcotics traffic. Countries in which illegal narcotics previously had been virtually unknown had become deeply involved. England, for example, historically a non-drug-consuming nation except for a few aesthetes, had become a consumer nation and now was suddenly finding itself to be a producer nation as well, notorious as a leading exporter of LSD. France and Italy, which historically had been "transit" nations between producer nations and consumer nations, were now discovering a wave of drug abuse among their own people, particularly the youth. Sweden, Switzerland, Finland, and Belgium, always regarded as sensible and industrious nations, had become youth centers for narcotics indulgence and illicit trafficking. Drug abuse by young people had attracted attention, but the startling extent of young people's involvement in trafficking was not yet common knowledge.

Dana Adams Schmidt, an American journalist, became interested in the young drug traffickers. He interviewed a group

of Americans arrested in Lebanon and reported that they were
of above-average intelligence, many of them university students. He also found them to be naive and somewhat pathetic
when they were caught, without much sense of the seriousness
of their acts. Even more revealing was their apparent ignorance; they had no idea that the Lebanese are old hands at the
smuggling game and have for centuries been detecting tricks
such as the ones they employed.

Why do young Americans, educated and from good families, indulge in such illegal activity as trafficking in hashish?
Some say it is just a lark, an adventure, while others say the
object is easy money. Traffickers often absolve themselves of
deeper guilt by asserting that in their opinion hashish is not a
dangerous drug. (That absolution is not claimed by those who
traffic regularly in heroin, since the horrors of heroin addiction are well publicized. Heroin smugglers frequently excuse
themselves on the ground that "if I didn't, someone else
would," or that they simply want the money.)

A California film writer who spent three years in a Beirut
prison claimed that he wasn't really guilty, that someone had
hidden narcotics in his car without his knowledge in the hopes
of recovering it secretly after he had driven out of the country.
Many young people, when apprehended, maintain stoutly that
they have been innocent victims of tricks by native merchants,
their fellow students, or devious tourists trying to use them
and protect themselves. One British student caught with
twenty-five pounds of hashish strapped around her body under
her clothing said her boyfriend made her do it. Other young-
sters said they were entrapped by merchants who sold them
double-bottom suitcases and then tipped off border guards in
order to claim a share of the fines imposed.

If a California film writer, foreign ambassadors, and traveling college students at first appeared to be unlikely partici-
pants in the international narcotics traffic, there have been
other surprises in recent years. David Anderson, a *New York*

Times reporter, described the mixed emotions that marked proceedings before a United States commissioner when Sybil Horowitz, thirty-four, mother of a fourteen-month-old child, was arraigned for her role as a member of an international gang carrying cocaine from Chile to New York. When taken into custody she had sobbed, "I want my baby to be with me." She had been paid $5,000 plus $2,000 expense money for each trip carrying narcotics to the United States.

The son of a Chicago banker, twenty-six-year-old Harvey Fleetwood, was arrested on charges of conspiracy to import hashish from India via Puerto Rico to the United States. Fleetwood's mixed bag of associates included a female student named Ziambardi, a free-lance TV cameraman named Goldberg, and several Syrians and Indians. Fleetwood himself worked as a newspaper reporter and had written, just before his arrest, an article about narcotics addiction based on interviews with a sixteen-year-old addict.

At the time of Interpol's report that world drug traffic had been revolutionized, American agents were regularly announcing increasing numbers of seizures. Such seizures seemed impressive, but in the context of the total problem, how far toward a solution did they progress? One way of measuring would be to recall Harold Munger, a "manufacturing wholesaler" who prepared heroin for sale to addicts until sentenced to prison for twelve to twenty years. (The conviction was later overturned on grounds that wiretap evidence had been used in the case.) Police reports announce the number of pounds of drugs they have confiscated in raids. A man like Munger will process what was originally one pound of pure heroin into about 42,000 individual doses.

The annual rate at which officials made seizures of smuggled heroin was nearly 312 pounds in fiscal 1969. Total annual illicit importation of heroin into the United States per year was then estimated at 5,000 to 6,000 pounds. Cut and packaged for sale by hundreds of underground businessmen like

Harold Munger, this would make from 200 million to a quarter of a billion doses. These statistics do not mean that efforts of the police were unavailing, but they do indicate that an understanding of the situation and the ultimate conquest of the drug problem requires much larger perspectives than the mere arrest of traffickers and seizure of their supplies.

The dimensions of the problem have increased geometrically during the years since Munger's arrest. It is possible, for example, to stash up to 150 pounds of powder in an automobile—hidden in the upholstery, under the fenders, or in tanks. Eighteen hundred private cars were shipped to the United States in 1971; new-car imports of Volkswagens, Peugeots, Citroens, BMWs, Fiats, and others total over a million a year. In Nice there are a number of "racing car" garages that will build in recesses and spaces for hiding narcotics on order.

Toward the end of August, 1970, United States, French, and Swiss agents broke up what was called the biggest smuggling operation on record. The operation was masterminded by three people based in Nice and Geneva. Two of the three were arrested. Since 1965 these three had shipped an estimated $500 million worth of heroin a year to the United States on scheduled international airliners. One of their methods was to hide the stuff in washrooms behind the towels. Pickups were made not at the gateway airports but at interior city landings.

On October 6, 1971, in France's biggest drug haul up to that time, André La Bay, a French businessman, was caught transporting 233 pounds of heroin in a rented car near Paris. His arrest was related to the breakup of a big narcotics ring. In September, 1971, United States customs agents intercepted a car that had been shipped to the United States from Europe with heroin hidden inside. The ring, subsequently destroyed, had smuggled 1,500 pounds of heroin into the country in 1970–71—one of the largest narcotics operations ever uncovered. On December 9, 1971, Antonio Seguara was sentenced to a long prison term for attempting to smuggle 206 pounds of heroin into the country in a Citroen. His codefendant turned state's evidence and revealed that Edmond Taillet, a French television performer, was to receive $1 million for his part in the scheme. The case alerted agents, who arrested two more traffickers in Puerto Rico with a Citroen holding 200 pounds and two more in Spain. They also seized another Citroen holding a cache of over 200 pounds of heroin.

It should be remembered that illicit heroin is only one of the narcotics coming into the United States. Others are the marijuana-hashish types, cocaine, and synthetics, imported and domestic. And the United States is only one country in which large-scale distribution of illicit drugs has become a fixture of daily life. A dozen other nations around the world are also seriously affected.

At Interpol headquarters there is a large wall map on which are marked the principal routes of the world narcotics traffic. The traffic moves across vast distances by land, sea, and air from producers to markets, and Group E is assigned to keep track of the international criminal sub-society occupied in this activity. Its facilities help national police forces close in on several sectors of a drug ring simultaneously.

For example, when narcotics courier Lucy Bradbie was caught red-handed at John F. Kennedy International Airport in New York, a telegram was received by another courier, Delia Morales, at a hotel in Santiago, Chile, warning her. It had been dispatched by an accomplice who saw from the airport visitors' observation deck that Lucy Bradbie was not getting through. The telegram advised Delia to abandon her luggage and run for it. The Chilean Interpol bureau, however, had received notices from New York and was one step ahead. Detectives were on hand as Delia left the hotel. They also picked up the ring's chief supplier and the chief of the South American end of the racket. In return, Interpol Chile notified

United States customs agents of the movements of South American ring members so that they could be picked up at several points around New York before anyone could sound the alarm.

Even a simple arrest requires this kind of cooperation. On May 28, 1967, two couriers traveling by Air France were arrested by customs agents in New York. Each was wearing a corset packed with six and one-half pounds of heroin. To accomplish the arrest, the police of Marseille and the Interpol Bureaus of France, Italy, and Canada had coordinated information with the United States Bureau of Narcotics. Through investigations after the arrests, the police agencies of the United States and Canada furnished information by which French police could arrest the accomplices in their country.

Beyond these exercises in coordination is a much deeper objective. The dynamics of international narcotics traffic requires constant reassessment, especially since economic prosperity and other social forces have accelerated the pace at which the use of narcotics is expanding. The picture is changing like a kaleidoscope. Prior to 1960, for example, hashish came into England from Nigeria, then from Burma. The traffic from India moved through merchant seamen working off freighters. Six rings operated out of Rangoon, dropping packets at ports of call on freighter routes such as Tilbury, Hull, and Glasgow. British and Indian law-enforcement officials cracked down. Simultaneously, British police raided a ship at Liverpool, seizing a 400-pound shipment and arresting seamen-couriers, while Burmese police arrested principal dealers in Rangoon. These arrests disrupted the traffic pattern, but almost at once a new pattern was organized from West Africa and Cyprus, with the Cyprus supplies drawn from Lebanon. This was displaced in about 1960 by traffic to England direct from Pakistan, organized by Pakistanis and Indians.

Interpol's 1966 General Assembly passed a resolution recommending that the worldwide campaign against the illicit drug traffic be intensified. The resolution congratulated Lebanon for measures it had taken toward eliminating the cultivation of cannabis by substituting other socially and economically beneficial crops. It suggested that other producing countries follow the examples of Morocco and Lebanon, which were the first to report constructive results in combatting cannabis. The 1967 General Assembly recommended that all Interpol members urge their governments to deal severely with pushers of cannabis and that its possession be confined to legitimate medical, scientific, and industrial use. The recommendations cited the Single Convention on Narcotic Drugs of 1961, which obligated the signatories to rigidly control cannabis, and the World Health Organization Expert Committee on Dependence-Producing Drugs, which had determined that cannabis can produce drug dependence.

This was the start of a new role for Interpol. It was now providing increased leadership toward a broader interpretation of police functions in crime prevention rather than sole emphasis on the apprehension of criminals. In the following year, 1968, the General Assembly passed two even stronger resolutions. The first again commended Lebanon for its efforts in a crop-substitution program and recommended that the United Nations agencies, particularly the Food and Agriculture Organization, give priority to technical assistance to Lebanon and to any other countries that were prepared to take similar steps. The second resolution pointed out that not all countries affiliated with Interpol were following through on former assembly resolutions covering drugs; called for better and quicker cooperation between national central bureaus and the General Secretariat; urged the Secretariat to work more closely with other agencies, in particular the United Nations agencies that were concerned with the drug program; urged member nations to pass national legislation to increase punishment for "growing, processing, transporting, selling or possessing drugs unlawfully" and to be more reluctant to grant bail or provisional release to anyone involved in the drug traffic. It also impressed upon affiliated countries the importance of adhering to international drug conventions, educating the public on the dangers of drug addiction, and destroying crops that produce drugs and substituting other crops.

Literally hundreds of names are applied to products derived from the Indian hemp plant that botanists call *Cannabis sativa* —marijuana, pot, hashish, reefer, joint. The male of the species is fibrous and can be manufactured into cord and rope; the female has tender leaves and flowering clusters that exude a resin. Depending on national custom or cultural pattern, the resin in the leaves and flowers is smoked or otherwise inhaled, eaten, or dissolved in liquid and drunk.

Cannabis is harvested wild or cultivated for local use on a small scale in most parts of the world. The plant had a large-scale introduction into the midwestern United States during World War II, when hemp imports were cut off and the government decided that we would grow our own to supply the navy with rope. The supplies of international traffickers, however, come from four principal growing areas: Lebanon, the interior of Mexico, Morocco, and the foothills of the Himalayas in Pakistan.

While most nations agreed to outlaw cannabis in 1925, major attention focuses on these four countries. Lebanon made an effort to induce mountain tribesmen to switch to sunflowers. The government subsidized them with seed, fertilizers, machinery, technical assistance, transport, and price supports two and one-half times the commercial market price. Starting in 1966 the Lebanese goal was to accomplish the switch of 75,000 acres from cannabis to sunflowers in three years. It reported initial success and a need for continuing effort in the suppression of cannabis. Meanwhile Lebanon's

military and political problems have diverted attention elsewhere.

Lebanon has long been a supplier to nations of the Middle
East and also to Europe. Students and tourists handle some of
this traffic, and migrant Turkish workers handle some. Bulk
shipments move by sea and air, concealed in freight, and by
private plane. The organizers use many amateurs and casual
smugglers, but traffic into Egypt, for example, apparently
requires professionals, especially since contraband must pass
through Israel, which has a strict policy against drugs. Egypt
takes about half of Lebanon's output; the balance goes to
Europe and the United States.

While American hippies have made themselves noticed in
Lebanon and in the cannabis traffic out of Beirut, the principal United States action is in Mexico, where at one time
more than 80 percent of the American cannabis supply
originated. The United States-Mexican border is 2,000 miles
long, providing ample opportunity for couriers to find illegal
crossing points. *Marijuana* is a Mexican word that originally
referred to poor-quality cigarettes; it now refers to any form of
the dried cannabis plant. Large fields of it are cultivated in
Chihuahua, Coahuila, Durango, and Zacatecas. Tons of the
plant are then moved to border towns such as Tijuana, Mex-
icali, and Nogales for transport across the line to California,
Arizona, New Mexico, and Texas. It usually is pressed into
one-kilo bricks, ready for sale to individuals for use by themselves and their friends or to professional dealers who ship in
volume for commercial distribution. Smugglers generally use
automobiles and conceal the marijuana in existing spaces or in
specially built compartments. For several years private
aircraft and boats have been increasingly pressed into service.
Sometimes a purchaser in the United States will arrange by
telephone for a seller in Mexico to meet him at an isolated
location along the border and to simply throw the marijuana
over the fence.

For wholesale shippers, getting over the frontier is only part of the work. Once into the country, the marijuana must be transported, usually by highway, to major cities—Los Angeles, San Francisco, Chicago, Detroit, New York— evading not only customs officials but also narcotics agents and state and local police. The masters of the wholesale traffic are Cubans, Puerto Ricans, and Mexicans. A majority of the couriers who work steadily in this traffic are Mexicans. Cubans had a big marijuana business going until Castro took power. When he shut it down abruptly, Cubans who were engaged in the trade simply shifted over to handling the Mexican product. Puerto Ricans developed a traffic in marijuana grown in Venezuela and Guiana and have also gone into Mexican markets.

Although Europeans get some of their cannabis from Lebanon, Morocco is handier. There it is grown in the mountains and brought by donkey and camel to Tangier, where a large, casual trade is carried on by Casbah merchants with flocks of German, British, and Scandinavian tourists and students. Knapsacks, hand luggage, autos, baskets, and other souvenirs are used to get the drug past Spanish customs and across homeland frontiers. Entrepreneurs have also attempted to organize a professional traffic by shipping to Spanish coastal towns from whence millions of European "customers" who travel and vacation there every year could carry it back to their home countries.

The fourth principal area producing for the international criminal traffic is Pakistan. England became the principal destination for its exported product, though some may be dropped off in West Germany or Belgium on the way, and some may be diverted to northern countries. The British-Pakistani axis, dating from about 1960, was said to have been established concurrently with a wave of Asian and West Indian immigration. After thousands of people from these lands started settling in London, Birmingham, Liverpool, and

other large population centers, Pakistani and Indian entrepreneurs formed them into a human pipeline for the transport of
cannabis into England.

Because of the distance, this traffic had to be in the form of
concentrated resin or hashish. It was organized to move
mainly by air and by private auto. New immigrants, both legal
and illegal, and former immigrants making trips home to visit
relatives were induced to carry concealed or camouflaged
packets of the drug. Either their trips were financed with this
understanding or they were paid set fees. On overland auto
trips, the hashish could be stashed in compartments, in spare
tires, or inside upholstery. Since large numbers of small con-
signments were being brought over, the traffickers could af-
ford to lose a percentage in customs seizures and charge it to
the cost of doing business.

Frankfurt and Brussels became staging points for the final
leg of the 4,000- or 5,000-mile journey. Couriers would take
it across the channel on car ferries or on commercial airliners.
British customs became very attentive, particularly to cars
driven off the ferries by Asians. In a typical instance, customs
officials stopped one car and virtually took it apart. They
found 119 pounds of hashish behind the door panels and the
back seat. The driver and passenger were Pakistanis.

As British customs pressure on travelers increased, the
Pakistani and Indian master traffickers shifted tactics to more
traditional methods, concealing hashish in merchandise and
ordinary cargo like crates of fruit, canned goods, and bulk
products coming by sea from Asia. In one notorious case a
brilliant Indian scientist residing in England and conducting
complex research projects at London University was found to
be devising schemes for smuggling cannabis from Pakistan.
His schemes included using a shipment of pickles and a shipment of rose-petal jam to smuggle more than 400 pounds of
cannabis resin worth over $350,000. But his arrest caused
little dent in the total traffic.

Once the hashish arrived safely in England, West Indians would take over, since they pretty much monopolized the network of consumer distribution. Native British criminals took no part in the drug traffic, and although there was talk of the American Mafia moving in, no evidence of this was available.

The 1969 General Assembly session zeroed in on heroin. The United States delegation reported on the growing heroin traffic in North America and the shifting patterns of transport to evade law-enforcement barriers. The United States delegation and delegations from France, Mexico, and Sweden proposed the most drastic resolutions ever placed before Interpol. The poppy-growing propensities of certain member nations were discussed more fully than ever before.

Heroin, morphine, and opium all derive from the poppy, a graceful, long-stemmed flower that is grown in a dozen or more countries. For the most part, growing and harvesting poppies is licensed by the government in certain countries, and much of the narcotics derived from them is produced legally. World production of opium for legitimate medical purposes was about 1,500 tons in 1971. The trouble comes from extra quantities that are produced for the most part by legal growers. Turkish farmers, for example, would harvest about 180 tons of opium legally each year and would secretly harvest an additional 30 to 80 tons that would disappear into the black market. Their motive was simple: what they sold privately brought $2.25 to $4.50 per pound more than what they sold officially. These extra few dollars per pound formed the foundation for a vast international business worth billions of dollars and employing thousands of members of the world's criminal sub-societies.

The leading countries in world production have been India and Russia, with Turkey third. Turkey and its poppies have been extremely important to the situation in the United States, as most of the illegal heroin in the United States has been originating as Turkish opium. Yugoslavia, Pakistan, Bulgaria, and Japan also are producers, as are Afghanistan and China. Mexico is a relative newcomer in poppy-growing, but its proximity to the American market is a powerful incentive. Iran resumed production in 1969 after a thirteen-year prohibition. Burma, Thailand, and Laos historically produced for the Asian trade until the Vietnam war brought thousands of potential American customers to their territories; then they began to seek a position in the United States market.

The illegal traffic begins quite simply. After the poppy flowers have lost their petals, there remain pods, which harden. The farmer makes an incision with a sharp knife in each pod and a milky juice oozes out. It dries on the pod overnight, turning brown and gummy. The farmer and his family scrape the dried juice from each pod and roll the scrapings into balls of several pounds weight and sell them, either to a legal purchaser or on the black market.

The present government of mainland China prohibits use of opium but licenses opium production for pharmaceutical use. During World War II, when the Chinese communities of the West Coast had difficulty importing opium from their mother country, some enterprising devotees of the stuff induced some Mexicans to try raising poppies and harvesting opium. The result was that Mexicans now have established an illegal opium industry of their own and are expanding it into a heroin trade.

A disturbing analysis of the emerging situation was discussed at the 1969 General Assembly. At the time, new patterns of drug traffic in the United States were bound to affect other nations. The boom in air travel had provided the drug smuggler with a new dimension. Couriers were not associated with the underworld and were not diplomats with baggage immunity. They were, Interpol had determined, average citizens —students, housewives, middle-class respectables, and airline personnel. The devices most commonly used were small bags attached to the body or secreted in body cavities.

Interpol had begun to keep special records on drug seizures, to chart patterns, and to circulate lists of identified traffickers. It now noticed an alarming expansion. Interpol listed 1,225 in 1966 and fewer than 1,500 in 1967, but by 1968 the list had grown to over 2,000, and in 1969 it had ballooned to over 3,500.

The heroin traffic is probably the most completely international of the world's criminal enterprises. Black-marketing Turkish farmers and brokers annually start tons of the raw opium on a route that circles halfway around the globe. It is carried across national frontiers by humans, donkeys, and camels, by auto and truck, aboard ship and aircraft. Along the way it is crudely converted by boiling it with slaked lime and ammonium calcium chloride into morphine base. The morphine base is dropped off at secret laboratories operating in southern France for refining into heroin, a fine white powder that is routed to the United States either directly or via Canada, Mexico, or South America. Importers then get it into the hands of brokers and wholesalers who in turn have it cut and packaged in plastic envelopes as individual doses for sale in streets and schoolyards, for use in ghetto flats and plushy apartments.

In the United States it is a billion-dollar criminal business. The New York end of it alone has been estimated to generate $219 million annually. Understandably, with this kind of money involved, there is a constant struggle by many eager opportunists to get into the act. Overseas the crude morphine used to move by sea to Marseille. There were historic ties to Beirut, one of the staging posts for opium and morphine from Turkey, dating back to the days when Lebanon was a French protectorate. More recently, since auto highways have been built across Europe, Turks have been using trucks and making connections in France through countries such as West Germany, Italy, and Switzerland. Even more influential have been migrations of labor. Turkish workers drawn to West European countries have set up community ties to the homeland and a courier service among migrants looking for a way to finance transportation to their jobs or for visits home.

Until the 1950s Corsicans and Sicilians dominated the European sector of the trade. Initially, they were middlemen, until the Corsicans moved into processing, took control of the clandestine laboratories around Marseille, and took control of export to the United States. The Sicilians had to be content with the American side of the business and stayed with it through underworld connections. Dominance of the heroin traffic by criminals loosely identified as members of "La Cosa Nostra," reported fairly strong until the middle 1960s, was challenged with growing ferocity by other ethnic groups— Blacks, Puerto Ricans, and Cubans—and reached crisis stages in New York politics when these groups started bidding for shares in political power.

Since those ethnic communities were supplying the bulk of the consumers, their leaders began demanding a larger share of control and profits. Cosa Nostra bosses were in something of a bind since Blacks, Puerto Ricans, and Cubans furnished a large sector of the distribution manpower as runners and pushers and inevitably forced their way into the packaging and wholesaling. Cosa Nostra members in the late 1960s reportedly had to make do with control of the bulk importing from overseas, which they hoped to hold because of their historic connections with suppliers in Italy and with Corsicans in France.

Since an important feature of this phase of the trade is financing, non-Italians began moving in simply because they were moneymen. South American, Cuban, and Jewish names periodically appear in news reports. Meanwhile, the Mexicans who were brought into poppy-growing to accommodate the United States West Coast Chinese during wartime have been operating their own laboratories to produce heroin and to pitch for a share of the market. They have yet to equal the

French in quality, but their supply lines are shorter, and some customers prefer the brown Mexican variety.

At one point in the 1960s there was an effort by Australians to get a piece of the lucrative American market by working with Black dealers directly, thus bypassing the Cosa Nostra. The enterprise failed when United States federal agents moved in to break up the ring through cooperation with the Australian Interpol bureau and police.

Generally, the Orient supplies its own regions, where the poppy has had devotees for thousands of years. In Thailand, Laos, and Burma, family farming yields an estimated 700 metric tons of opium per year to supply several million addicts of the Far East and Southeast Asia. For them it provides their only cash income, and it also provides wealth for certain native generals who direct the trade out of Laos and Burma. Opium-smoking traditionally has been the chosen addiction in Hong Kong, Singapore, and Bangkok, but recently, there has been a switch toward morphine and heroin.

United States agents started watching for signs of a move toward the American market from the Orient. Hong Kong, particularly, could be a staging post for clandestine shipments to the West Coast. Meanwhile, Asians had their own addicts to supply. Hong Kong, for instance, had a reported 150,000 addicts in a population of 4 million, but the United States has a population of over 220 million and 250,000 to 500,000 addicts, according to some official estimates. In addition to Hong Kong, there are large numbers of addicts in Thailand, Malaysia, Australia, and Japan to be taken care of by the traffickers of the Far East. The American market, however, is considered the jackpot, and with the opening of the decade of the 1970s American agents detected the beginnings of a connection between the masters of the Oriental traffic and those of the pipelines from France.

Japan represents another new force in the criminal narcotics traffic. Until recently, Japanese were nonusers as a nation. Their former involvement was strictly in trading. When they took Manchuria in the 1930s, the Japanese took control of poppy cultivation and the opium traffic based on it. After World War II, as Japan succeeded in achieving affluence, high employment, and broadly based prosperity, widespread narcotics addiction began. The addicts generally preferred expensive, high-quality heroin, mirroring the American taste rather than the opium preference of other Orientals. Prices in Japan reached the level of the American market, a kilo of heroin selling wholesale for around $27,000 and retail for about $83,000 to $250,000, depending on the supply and the state of police suppression. Traffic was organized out of Hong Kong and Bangkok with laboratories in Hong Kong and Macao, which were said to produce quality comparable to the European.

Interpol's 1969 General Assembly met in an atmosphere of crisis. The enormous growth of the United States market plus the years of economic prosperity in western Europe, Japan, and other areas had greatly stimulated levels of criminal activity. If Interpol's list accurately reflected the number of professional big-time narcotic traffickers, there was a 75 percent increase in one year. It also demonstrated that where previously French traffickers had dominated the international scene, now many other nationalities were represented.

Interpol began to assume a new posture. To its responsibility for straight police work it added moral force for establishing strong countermeasures, offering itself as a leader of world thinking that might mobilize civilized society for action. As police cooperated with national central bureaus to exert pressure on traffickers, they traced the continuously changing pattern of activity in the trade. Interpol specialists marked the spread of cannabis in western Europe. The synthetic drug traffic, which Interpol had been observing previously, was found to be taking hold in European countries; amphetamines in Sweden; LSD in Denmark, France, Germany, Spain, Sweden, and the United Kingdom.

At the assembly meeting it became clear that in addition to

the vast growth of heroin abuse in the United States, there was a burgeoning abuse of cocaine and continual expansion in the use of marijuana. Interpol declared that drug abuse had become epidemic throughout the world and sounded an alarm to which national governments began to listen with new interest. Interpol's sole power is to assess and articulate. After that, it is up to its delegates to urge their national governments to advise participation in intensely concerted action against the drug menace.

At that same assembly four key resolutions of astonishing forcefulness for the time were passed. They were developed in close collaboration with the United Nations Commission on Narcotic Drugs and outlined a drastic process for coming to grips with the narcotics problem:

Wherever illegal cultivation of opium poppy, cannabis, or coca plants is found, the land known to have been used for that purpose should be confiscated; where needed, the assistance of the nation's armed forces should be used in the destruction of such crops.

This action, the resolutions stated, should be in addition to all other punitive measures imposed by law for illicit cultivation. Further, stringent restrictions should be placed on travel and immigration to countries that have opium poppy or cannabis under cultivation legally or illegally, and all persons, especially young people, should be excluded if they are reasonably suspected of being involved in traffic in narcotic drugs or psychotropic substances.

The resolutions further recommended that the national central bureau in each country urge its government to prohibit cultivation of poppy and cannabis and that steps be taken by whatever legal means are appropriate in each country— including the organization of special squads assigned to suppression of narcotics offenses, training courses for law-enforcement officers, increased use of technological means to detect and destroy illicit crops, and appropriation of adequate funds for equipment where necessary to carry out these measures.

Linked to these measures, Interpol proposed, should be those needed for humane handling of the health, social, and economic aspects of the problem. It proposed:

That a clear distinction be made in penal law and penitentiary practice between occasional users and persons deeply involved in illicit traffic; that traffickers should be subject to heavy prison sentences to keep them from being a danger to society; that addicts and persons found in possession of small quantities for personal use should be allowed to benefit from all systems of parole suited to their cases, especially if they are minors or first offenders.

To deal with the economic dislocations that result from the eradication and prohibition of poppy and cannabis cultivation, Interpol recommended that the alternative policy of introducing substitute crops become general practice.

It further proposed that each country impose strict control measures on the distribution of psychotropic drugs within its borders, making them available to users only upon medical prescription and prohibiting unauthorized possession for distribution. All producers should be licensed; trade should be limited to authorized persons; and transactions at all stages, from production to retail distribution, should be supervised.

Next on the Interpol roster for concern and intense action was cocaine.

One of the new forces at work in the ever-shifting patterns of the narcotics traffic was the growing American taste for cocaine. Coming exclusively from South America, cocaine changed the world drug traffic pattern. As a result, there are possibilities for underdeveloped nations to get a larger piece of the action. Cocaine—the "rich man's drug," "the society drug," "Charley," or "C"—is derived from the leaves of the coca plant. Cocaine's pristine whiteness has led to the name "snow." Another of its names, "coke," is a reminder that it was once, though no longer, an ingredient of the soft drink by which America is identified around the world.

Cocaine has been the subject of mystery and mythology. In the past decade it has also made a striking comeback in popular interest after a half-century of obscurity.

In 1968 Interpol learned of the discovery of twenty-one cocaine laboratories in Bolivia and Peru. In 1969 several more were found. Interpol called attention to the fact that cocaine smugglers were following the practice of heroin traffickers who were reported in 1965 to be using international airlines for transport. They, too, were concealing packages of drugs behind panels in the washrooms of airliners that were going on to inland airports. Once the smuggler had passed customs inspection at the port of entry, he proceeded on his flight to his inland destination and dropped off his delivery.

South America probably has the world's largest concentration of drug users. In the central region of South America, the numbers are variously estimated at 8 million to 15 million people. For 1,000 years or more, cocaine has been a local matter for the natives in this region.

Today, however, cocaine looks like the fastest-growing addictive drug on the international traffic scene. As recently as 1967, after a two-year study, President Lyndon B. Johnson's National Crime Commission Report, in its lengthy chapter on narcotics, devoted exactly six and one-half lines to cocaine, summarizing, "At present it is not the major drug of abuse it once was." In that same year customs and narcotics agents seized forty-eight pounds of pure cocaine, equivalent to about $18 million worth of sales. Obviously, the cocaine traffic at the time of the official study was rapidly accelerating. The total illicit quantity entering the United States was estimated at between 600 and 1,000 pounds in 1967, compared with a total of ten ounces seized a decade earlier. By 1969 the quantity seized doubled—to between 1,000 and 2,000 pounds. According to the experts' rule of thumb, those seizures represented between 5 and 10 percent of the total quantity smuggled.

The master traffickers in cocaine were from Cuba and Puerto Rico; an upswing in the use of cocaine was noticeable in the mid-1950s, coincident with a wave of immigration from those islands. Prior to the mid-1950s the American Mafia had been entrenched in Cuba with a franchise to operate gambling there. During this period they had an opportunity to instruct the natives in the details of the heroin traffic. The Cubans were independent, however, and developed the beginnings of an international cocaine traffic based in the islands of the Caribbean. When Batista was ousted and Castro came to power, the Mafia was kicked out, the Cuban drug traffickers migrated to Florida and New York, and the growing cocaine traffic was transferred with them.

Unlike the complex web of syndicates that conducted the international heroin traffic, the cocaine traffic was extraordinarily simple. A complete smuggling ring can function with fewer than a half-dozen people and can be started by two partners, or even by one mastermind with two lieutenants. It can even be run as a family enterprise like an old-time candy store.

A typical international ring was that of Ralph Santana, working with two henchmen, Lionel Marquez and Frank Serrano. Until arrested, Serrano handled the South American end in Chile, out of Santiago and Valparaiso. He assembled supplies, briefed couriers, taught them the tricks needed to get through United States customs, scheduled their trips, and coordinated with associates in North America. Marquez managed the United States end, directing the couriers' clandestine delivery and distribution to wholesalers in Miami and New York.

Santana handled the financing and policy-making for the enterprise while his wife, Lilian, was in charge of recruiting the women couriers, fitting them with specially-designed undergarments and double-bottom suitcases in which they were taught to carry cocaine. The ring bought their supplies from a dealer in Chile—René Hard or René Hard-Huasseff. In 1964, when the American market was just beginning to swing, this one group in a six-month period brought $15 million to $25 million worth of cocaine into the United States.

These family-type operations are quickly broken up once the first lead is uncovered. In busting the Santana ring, the Interpol bureau in Chile worked with United States customs and narcotics agents in Miami, Brooklyn, Manhattan, and Long Island. The break in the case came in 1964, when one of the ring's couriers, Lucy Juanita Bradbie, looked "nervous" to a customs officer at John F. Kennedy International Airport. He asked her to open her suitcase, and his practiced eye told him that it had a double bottom. Lucy Bradbie was detained, and in five or six days principals as well as couriers were under lock and key from Manhattan to Oyster Bay to Santiago. Of the family "insiders," Santana, Serrano, Marquez, and their wives, only Santana got away, to be captured later and given a fifteen-year sentence.

The traffic grows, however, because such simple arrangements can be replaced. While some operators like the fast action of airplanes, others prefer less spectacular cargo boats, whose crew members work as couriers out of Lima and other South American ports. Some bring supplies over the Pan American Highway to Ecuador for shipping out, while still others move it through Venezuela to Caracas and then by sea or air to Miami.

There is a side track to Europe and the Middle East that takes cocaine into southern France and Lebanon for distribution. Lebanese traffickers handle this as a sideline; some heroin users like to blend in a little cocaine. There has also been observed a three-point voyage pattern, linking eastern

Mediterranean ports, Florida, and Brazil. Florida yachts pick up cocaine in Brazil and deliver it in the eastern Mediterranean, then pick up hashish there or heroin in France or Spain for delivery in Florida, where the triangle is started again.

A much larger effect on the international criminal traffic pattern seems to be building up via Mexico. Cocaine has been moving from Chile, Peru, and Equador to ports in western Mexico by boat or to Mexico City by airliner. It is then smuggled overland up to Guadalajara, and from there it is distributed along the heroin network of the United States-Mexican border towns. Here, too, heroin dealers started handling cocaine as a sideline, but apparently it is becoming a fixture of the clandestine traffic. One advantage is price, since pure cocaine wholesales at 20 percent less coming this route than by way of New York.

Even more striking is the effect of cocaine on the criminal narcotics traffic in New York and other northern American cities. With Cubans and Puerto Ricans operating their own rackets based on coca, the monolithic hold of the Cosa Nostra groups based on heroin became eroded in the criminal subsocieties. Ethnic solidarity in the ghettos gave the Latins their base, while pressure from the Black community for a piece of the action in heroin gained results, since Blacks provided a massive number of customers. From being pushers, the Blacks moved into packaging and wholesaling in tandem while the Puerto Ricans and Cubans took on heroin as a sideline to cocaine. In the face of this pressure, Cosa Nostra groups retreated and relinquished most of the traffic below the importer level. Even in this, however, they are apparently having to share with individuals from a variety of ethnic origins.

At Brussels in 1970 the General Assembly again found it necessary to pass resolutions concerning the growing drug problem. This time the concern was particularly with the mind-altering and psychotropic drugs. The General Assembly recommended that all Interpol member nations fully support an upcoming United Nations plenipotentiary conference scheduled for Vienna in February, 1971, to discuss bringing these drugs under international control. The alarm that Interpol was raising over the spread of synthetic drugs seemed to be fully justified. Interpol placed the synthetics among the substances that were contributing to the epidemic proportions of the worldwide drug problem and urged that they be treated with the same levels of controls and countermeasures as had been instituted against the natural narcotic drugs.

"Bennies," "goofballs," "speed," and "sleepers" are a few of the names given to synthetic drugs. They are generally classified as "psychotropics" and are of three types: stimulants (benzedrine, amphetamines), tranquilizers (barbiturates), and halucinogens (LSD, often called "acid"). Unlike the botanical drugs, the synthetics became identified as essentially belonging to the "youth scene," a sort of cultural enclave in which young people have marked out a domain.

Denmark and Sweden became principal European markets for the synthetics. The United States is the primary target for an international criminal traffic. Much of the crime involved, however, is local and amateur. Thefts from drugstores and from pharmaceutical warehouses and factories became a major source in some communities. A couple of small boxes contain thousands of doses, so theft is attractive.

At one point England unexpectedly found itself experiencing this kind of crime for local consumption. It also became an exporter of LSD to the American market and an importer-consumer of hashish and heroin. Clandestine laboratories in and around London became producers of LSD.

LSD became very disturbing to law-enforcement people because so much can be done with so little. A droplet is a dose. One gram, equal to 5,000 doses, can be carried in a lipstick holder and can generate perhaps $12,500 in retail sales. A kilogram, equivalent to 5 million doses, can be carried like a couple of bottles of liquor and would be worth $2 million at wholesale rates.

On the other hand, traffic in LSD required as much as $5,000 to $10,000 to start a lab and $540 for a single gram of the basic material, ergotoxine. By comparison, youngsters trafficking in synthetics can go into pills on a shoestring. The profits are smaller, but so is the investment. An enterprising youth could buy a hundred pills for a few dollars and double his money by retailing them for higher prices. Or, with a relatively small amount of capital, say $1,500, he could buy 50,000 Preludin tablets in Switzerland or Italy, smuggle them into Sweden, and double his money by wholesaling. Or he could multiply his return five-fold or eight-fold by retailing.

The European market is unusual. It developed partly as a by-product of a rootless community comprising American military deserters and draft-dodgers and alienated youth of all nations. It was ironic that Scandinavia should become the home for pill addicts, since those countries rigorously control the manufacture and distribution of psychotropic pharmaceuticals. All supplies had to be smuggled from Switzerland, Italy, or other nearby countries. Copenhagen became the hub of auto, air, and ferry traffic. Traffic was moving to market in Denmark by auto, by ferry to Malmö, and by airline to Stockholm. In 1970 Sweden was reported to have 10,000 to 12,000 addicts swallowing methedrine and shooting amphetamines—usually Preludin dissolved in water and injected by hypodermic. Denmark was reported to have 4,000 persons taking amphetamines.

But the major action in pill traffic became the 2,000-mile United States-Mexican border and a network of traffic lanes handling marijuana, heroin, and other drugs. The United States Bureau of Customs, which first kept records on pills in

1968, found 525 cases of smuggling and seized 3,900,000 pills. In 1969, 630 cases of smuggling were discovered, and 4,631,925 pills were seized.

Border town drugstores are big outlets. A young man in October, 1969, told the House of Representatives Select Committee on Crime that he had simply walked into a drugstore and purchased 300,000 barbiturates. Mexicans buy in million-pill quantities from United States pharmaceutical firms for secret export back to the U.S. In July, 1968, a Chicago firm, Bates Laboratories, shipped 1,200,000 psychotropic pills to a Mexican "company" whose business address, a Narcotics Bureau investigator found, was "on the site of the eleventh hole of the Tijuana Country Club golf course." Actual delivery was made in care of an export-import agent at the border with instructions to hold the merchandise there for a Mexican pickup. This shipment was confiscated, and the drug firm admitted that it had been doing business with the same nonexistent company for ten years.

Evidently traffickers were making use of the "bonded warehouse" trick to save time and transport and to evade customs. A Mexican resident, under cover of owning a drugstore or simply by having pharmaceutical company stationery printed, would place an order with an American drug firm and request delivery at a bonded warehouse in a United States border town. He would drive across the border checkpoint, pick up his order, and record the export transaction. On the way back from the warehouse, however, before recrossing the frontier, he would drop off the shipment by prearrangement with an American trafficker. Other traffickers were using automobiles and small private planes as in the heroin, marijuana, hashish, and cocaine traffic. Pills sometimes became a sideline for traffickers in the other narcotics products. Interpol reported that the synthetics also were smuggled in fishing vessels and power boats, which were coming into greater use. Triangle shipping routes reminiscent of the seventeenth century rum and slave trade had come to life again as a cocaine and heroin track: South America to southern Europe to North America.

Overall, adding the twentieth-century phenomenon of synthetic drugs to the vast botanical production has meant that even the former limitations of climate and geography are no longer a restraining influence. Viewed globally, world population has been thrusting toward a common experience in drug experimentation and addiction at the end of the 1960s. If the term *revolution* is apt, it is apt not only in terms of the growth and acceleration of drug production, traffic, and consumption, but also in terms of basic changes in the patterns of these activities. Interpol's reports and resolutions pressed upon society the urgent need to confront this hard fact.

Meanwhile, social, economic, and political forces continued to present their unresolved dilemma. In Brazil, Turkey, Lebanon, Peru, Kashmir, Bolivia, and other areas, large sectors of the citizenry earn their daily bread by cultivating crops that provide the narcotics that cause the deterioration and death of the citizenry in other nations.

In Turkey, for example, at about the time Interpol and the United States were becoming aroused over the enormity of the problem, more than 100,000 households were engaged in poppy cultivation. The welfare of these families and the stability of political parties in government for whom they voted had to be taken into account when analyzing the problem. In planning strategies against narcotics abuse, Interpol found that the interrelationships of the illicit drug traffic with the social, economic, and political affairs of many nations proved to be wide, deep, and complex.

The United States came to the same conclusion when it started to intensify its own actions. The lesson was driven home on April 5, 1971, when a customs inspector in New Jersey, Lynn Pelletier, decided to spotcheck a VW camper. It was on the Elizabeth city docks waiting to be picked up by its owner, a Frenchman who was standing by. Mrs. Pelletier said she decided to examine the vehicle "on a hunch." She made a

routine inspection, looking for broken seams in the upholstery, scratched metal, and other signs of tampering, and
turned up ninety-six pounds of heroin stashed in the plastic
water tank and under the floorboards.

The Frenchman was arrested on the spot and lodged in the
Somerset County jail with bail set at $500,000. He turned out
to be Roger Xavier Leon Delouette, a former agent in a
French counterespionage service called the Service Documentation Extérieure et Contra Espionage. Delouette insisted that
he had been the tool of a Max Fournier, who, he said, had induced him to smuggle the heroin from France into the United
States. Delouette had been given $5,500 in francs to purchase
and ship the camper and was promised $50,000 on delivery.

The plot thickened when it developed that Fournier was a
colonel in French counterintelligence and that he was
allegedly involved in the kidnapping of Algerian leader Ben
Barka. According to Delouette, who gave a detailed statement
to United States Attorney General Herbert J. Stern, the colonel had recruited him on December 15, 1970. Following instructions, Delouette had bought the camper in mid-March
and had had it shipped to the United States. Still acting under
instructions, he flew to New York in April on the day before
he was arrested, registered in a New York hotel, and waited
for his contact on the receiving end of the drop, who was to
pay him. The contact, he said, was in the French consulate in
New York.

During the investigations that followed on both sides of the
Atlantic, the governments of both countries became involved
through their embassies, judicial officials, and political parties.
A feud among members of the French counterespionage appa-
ratus was aired, including charges that intelligence agents
were engaged in narcotics and counterfeit traffic. This is a
facet of the narcotics problem in which Interpol cannot
become involved, although it continues to play an active role
in "straight" criminal traffic.

On the morning of August 29, 1970, a privately owned two-engine prop Martin 202 landed on a freshly bulldozed landing strip in a remote hashish-producing area in Lebanon near Baalbek. It carried $51,532 in cash. Waiting for the plane were fifteen Lebanese and a large tractor-drawn trailer pulled up at a loading platform. On the trailer were sixty sacks of hashish. In charge were five Americans who planned to buy three tons of hashish for $90,000 and resell it in the United States for an estimated $3 million.

Interpol, which tracked the entire caper, alerted the police agencies in each of the countries involved. The five had originally met in Amsterdam and flown to Nicosia, Cyprus, where they filed a flight plan to either Athens or Naples direct. When they took off, however, they flew toward Lebanon. With Interpol directing operations, the Nicosia air controllers tracked the Martin on their radar screens. At the same time Interpol Cyprus sent an alert to Interpol Beirut requesting Beirut air controllers to pick the plane up on their radar. The pilot of the Martin, however, flew low, evaded Beirut radar, and disappeared. The Lebanese police immediately began a countrywide search. A police patrol located the Martin in the field near Baalbek. The hashish was being loaded while the plane stood by with its engines running. The police moved in and a running gun battle ensued. By that time thirteen sacks weighing 1,412 pounds were already loaded. The five Americans scrambled into the plane amid a hail of bullets and took off, leaving forty-seven sacks and their Lebanese colleagues to the police.

Lebanese air force jets scrambled after the Martin but lost track of it. The smugglers flew an evasive course over the Mediterranean. Airports throughout the eastern Mediterranean region were alerted via the Interpol network. Nicosia airport, the first to have traced the Martin, sent out a missing aircraft alert, and Beirut identified it as a fugitive aircraft. Among the airports that were warned was the one at Candia on the island of Crete. Six minutes after they were notified, a radio request came in to the control tower asking permission to land and refuel. The pilot said he was flying a Convair 240. Thirteen minutes later a Martin 202 landed and taxied off the landing runway. A steamroller meandered out to block its path. The five in the plane were arrested after Interpol Washington helped identify them. The pilot was former United States Air Force Lieutenant Colonel John R. Moore. The other four were Philip Amos of Sacramento, David Mantell and Kenneth H. Connel, both of San Francisco, and Robert Black.

Alert at last to the complexity of the social, political, and economic problems involved in drug trafficking, the United States has mounted a historic effort to confront it with massive activities on several fronts. At the same time it has recognized that efforts of this sort can only be effective if they are carried out with an eye to the capabilities of Interpol. Since 1969 the United States has intensified its level of participation in Interpol and in international organizations that collaborate with Interpol; 1969 was the year Iran resumed opium production.

In addition to moving on diplomatic, economic, and educational fronts, the United States has been following a pattern set by Interpol, and it has been pursuing programs of international cooperation, particularly with France, Mexico, and Turkey.

In France, where clandestine laboratories process the heroin that supplies the American market, American and French representatives have met to discuss effective crackdowns. The ability of those laboratories to escape detection has been widely publicized. Much less publicized has been the fact that France was conducting its battle against drugs with four police officers assigned to the Marseille area and fewer than fifty more throughout the country. France announced that it would add two dozen special narcotics police in Marseille and three hundred more in other sections of the country.

Perhaps what Interpol regarded as the revolutionary turn in the world of drugs contributed to this decision. France had always been a "transit" country for the drug trade, without its own people becoming addicted. In 1969, however, it became public knowledge that the nation had quietly acquired a problem of its own, especially among young people and the middle class. An estimated 30,000 addicts were reported, largely favoring hashish and marijuana. The experiences of other countries were not hard for the French to interpret—addicts progressed from cannabis to hard drugs—and France had a reputation for producing the finest heroin, and Iran had new opium tonnage to get rid of.

American government officials said they had been trying for fifteen years to get the French to crack down thoroughly on heroin laboratories. In 1970 the French said they really meant business. The number of French narcotics police and agents was increased, and all police officers concerned with drugs underwent new training. By late 1971 France had seventy-five narcotics agents operating in the Marseille-Nice region. Periodically, there are reports of new secret laboratories in Switzerland, Belgium, and West Germany, and there are seizures in these countries. Should the French labs be eliminated, international cooperation will still be needed to keep replacements from springing up in other countries of Europe and the Far East.

From 1960 to the end of the decade, French police had closed five secret laboratories operating around Marseille. After that they became more aggressive, and, aided by Interpol, they shut down five more labs in a twelve-month period during 1971-72.

Meanwhile, the officials of the United States and Mexico seem to have reached an understanding. A "border war" against narcotics smuggling was staged in the autumn of

1969, complete with military nomenclature—Operation Intercept. It succeeded in drawing attention to the Mexican interior, where cannabis and poppies were being cultivated. Mexico pledged to increase efforts at destroying these crops before or after harvesting to keep as much marijuana, hashish, and heroin as possible off the American market. United States officials practiced the finest of press agentry in order to induce Mexican cooperation. They started thorough inspection procedures that interrupted the flow of frontier traffic and had the border-town merchants screaming with rage, since their prosperity was founded on this traffic. The Customs Bureau then announced that it would release for publication the names of twenty Mexican citizens indicted for violations of American narcotics laws. The Mexicans doubtless remembered the embarrassment of having Salvator Pardo-Bolland, the Mexican Ambassador to Bolivia, arrested, tried, convicted, and jailed for working in the drug traffic. Mexican diplomacy went to work in Washington, and Mexicans pledged intensified control. Washington, in turn, agreed not to expose the identity of this group. The eradication of crops and the destruction of harvests was assigned to the Mexican army. Many Mexican generals, however, are powerful figures in provincial politics, and the results were not entirely predictable.

Operation Intercept ended with the ceremonial burning of several tons of marijuana while Mexican and American officials looked on. It was followed in 1970 by Operation Cooperation, which was aimed at getting the Mexican police to intensify their antidrug activities. It resulted in more arrests being made by the Mexican police, more seizures of marijuana, and the burning of some poppy fields. Aided by a United States grant of $1 million earmarked for the purchase of five helicopters, three airplanes, and other equipment, the Mexican army put about 10,000 soldiers into antidrug work. By 1971 they had destroyed more than 9,000 poppy fields with a total area of about 6,000 acres.

Turkey was the third target in this diplomatic offensive. Turkey's production and illegal export had boomed in the 1960s as a result of Iran's noble experiment in stopping poppy cultivation. Turkish opium held the lion's share of the rich and highly prized American heroin market. Until 1970 Turkey supplied about half the opium smuggled into Iran.

In 1969 the United States made a $3 million loan to Turkey to aid in getting farmers to switch from poppies to other crops. Turkey ordered acreage reduced and said that poppy-growing would be permitted in only nine instead of seventeen provinces. Farmers made up the difference in production by more intensive cultivation. The United States sent negotiators in 1970 to obtain further commitments for cuts in production. By then Iran was adding 500 or 600 tons to the world's opium supply. Iran pledged to resume the ban on its production if its neighbors, Turkey and Afghanistan, would do so. The United States gave Turkey a $40 million development loan, but Iran could not help noticing that no strings were attached that required Turkey to reduce opium production. Turkey was important to the North Atlantic Treaty Organization. It is strategically located at the eastern end of the Mediterranean, where Arab-Israel tensions were simmering and where the Soviet Union was expanding its naval and military presence. Diplomatic negotiations with Turkey regarding opium were fitted into an overall framework of United States-Turkish relations.

In June, 1971, the United States obtained from Turkey a formal commitment by treaty to end poppy cultivation after the 1972 season. In 1971, 100,000 farmers applied to the Turkish government for licenses to grow opium poppies, an increase of 20,000 over the previous year. In 1972, it was estimated, 150,000 licenses would be requested. The United States pledged compensation to poppy farmers, a powerful incentive in itself for applying to the government for licenses. This could be an expensive commitment that may not be limited to the Middle East. Sixty percent of the world's opium is reported to be grown in the rugged Shan states of Burma and in the remote mountain regions of Laos and Thailand. It was assumed that traffickers would look to these sources if the Middle East supply were reduced or cut off.

The United States has made a signal effort to live up to the spirit and letter of recent Interpol resolutions on the drug problem. President Nixon, in a special message to Congress in June, 1971, requested $155 million in antidrug appropriations, including $7.5 million for investigations, $18 million for customs, $1 million to train narcotics police of other nations, and $2 million for research on herbicides to eradicate narcotics-producing plants. The special message also established a cabinet-level Special Action Office of Drug Abuse Prevention to be headed by Psychopharmacologist Dr. Jerome Herbert Jaffe of the University of Chicago. The office was established to oversee, coordinate, and lead the national effort to combat the drug problem.

The same message designated the drug problem as a "national emergency" and stated that, in the President's opinion, "the only really effective way to end heroin traffic is to end opium production and the growing of poppies." The President declared that he would propose the eradication of the opium poppy as an international goal and directed that research efforts to find synthetic medical substitutes for opium derivatives be intensified.

In January, 1972, the President added another high-level post to conduct the war on drug abuse, a special assistant attorney general in charge of drug law enforcement on the community level. He appointed Myles J. Ambrose, the former head of the United States Bureau of Customs.

In its last year of full-scale opium production before the official ban, Iran had an addict population of 2 million. After seven years of opium prohibition, the number had decreased to 35,000. It is astonishing that American authorities did not inquire into the secret behind this extraordinary achievement in dealing with drug addiction. A newspaper report said that clinics were set up around the country to help addicts kick the habit. They probably cost considerably less than the $50.5 million that New York spent in 1965–1969 to get 150 addicts cured.

10
Interpol
and the Future

Eᴀʀʟʏ in July, 1965, a house in Bienne, Switzerland, was burglarized. The front door and four interior doors were forced open with a crowbar and a screwdriver. Inside the house investigators found several kinds of prints. On the doors were tool markings. On the floors were prints made by rubber soles that did not match the shoes of any person who lived in the house. Around the house were some fingerprints, part of a glove print, and, on the main door frame, the outlines of a right and left ear. The ear prints were transferred onto paper.

Later that month two men were arrested in the act of breaking into another house. On them were found a specially adapted chisel and screwdriver that left marks that compared with the tool marks found in the house in Bienne. The sole prints matched the sole of one of the men's shoes. The evidence that clinched the case, however, was the ear prints. By comparing ear prints of both men with those found at the

Bienne house, the police were able to prove conclusively that the ear prints were made by one of them.

In a sense one might say that ear printing, like fingerprinting, has arrived. It is now possible to identify a criminal not only by his fingerprints but also by the mark of his ear. The position of the ear prints found in Bienne indicated that the culprit had leaned against the door frame and left an inadvertent calling card.

At first this method of criminal identification may seem surprising. Actually, however, the scientific and theoretical basis for it was developed some time ago. A. A. Reiss, head of the photographic laboratory at Lausanne University, wrote, in a book entitled *Portrait Parle: Méthode Alphonse Bertillon*, "The ear is the most distinguishing feature of the human face. With its many cavities and undulations, there is such a wide variety of possible structures that it is almost impossible to find two persons whose ears are exactly identical in all their parts. Moreover, the shape of the ear does not alter from birth to death."

Professor A. Niceforo of Naples and Brussels Universities wrote, in *La Police et L'Enquête Judiciare Scientifique (The Police and Scientific Criminal Investigation)*, "The ear is the most important element of the description. It is the organ which provides the greatest numbers of precise distinguishing marks. Shapes and forms vary widely from person to person and there is absolute invariability in each individual; this means that an exact description of the parts of the ear could in itself be enough to establish the identity of a person."

In still another work on the identification of criminals, Dr. Edmond Locard writes, "This organ, the part of the face which is given the least attention in everyday life, is the most important in scientific police work, because it is the most distinctive. The ear possesses the two fold advantage of being invariable in its proportions and shape, from birth to death, and of being so varied that it is impossible to find two identical ears."

This new wrinkle in criminal identification, still in the process of experimentation and development, is only one of the many innovations in police techniques that Interpol reports to its members in the pages of its publications. Another is the use of voiceprints, the identification of individuals through the characteristic electronic prints of their voices. Voiceprints are used increasingly against extortionists, blackmailers, and other criminals whose primary instrument is the telephone. A good deal of experimentation and refinement will be necessary before this method will rate with fingerprinting in the technology of criminal justice, but a scientific basis has already been developed.

Science and theory are due to play a much larger role in the future—in the use of computers, for example. In 1970 fifteen Interpol members reported that their police forces were using computers; eight others reported that they were planning to introduce them. At present their main uses seem to be for keeping statistics, recording data, handling traffic problems, assisting in the control of firearms, tracing stolen property, and keeping tabs on criminal modus operandi.

These uses are among the more simple, however; much larger dimensions are exemplified in the application of electronic data technology to crime syndicate investigations, using computer analysis to unravel intricately concealed financial affairs and business associations.

The use of new techniques and methods is by no means the exclusive domain of forces of law. Criminals and criminal sub-societies are changing their targets and modus operandi to take new developments into account. For instance, the Durham Gang used computers in a large-scale swindle of the New York City government. The gang programmed a check-printing machine to spout a stream of checks made out to fictitious persons—and the gang members cashed the checks. Another group adapted Wall Street's stock transfer system for a swindle of $4 million worth of securities, which they siphoned out of brokerage houses into their own bank accounts in Switzerland, California, and Georgia. The notorious Rosenbaum-Stone group used Swiss banking, set up a string of dummy corporations, and swindled the United States government by $4 million worth of fake invoices for nonexistent materials and work on naval contracts.

These are a few indications of the ways in which the world of crime has changed in the half century since Interpol was founded in Vienna. To the layman, the policeman's job is still that of catching the crook or stopping him before he commits another crime. In modern times this takes the policeman into fields he never dreamed of fifty years ago.

At a meeting of the heads of Interpol national central bureaus in December, 1968, the delegate from Ceylon introduced a resolution calling for cooperation in the enforcement of currency exchange controls. The Guatemalan delegate concurred, saying that exchange control violations were occurring in many Latin American countries, including his own. Not long before, accounting documents and authorizations for foreign exchange had been presented to banks in Guatemala and had been found to be forgeries. In other cases swindlers had succeeded in obtaining and using the official stamps of exporting countries. The effect of these violations of exchange control agreements and laws was to devalue currency.

As international trade continues to increase, the incidence of rackets and schemes that take advantage of trade volume or that find ways to evade exchange control regulations will doubtless proliferate.

The range of the modern policeman's concern seems fantastic compared with that of even one short decade ago, both quantitatively and qualitatively. The resolutions at Interpol

General Assemblies are one indication, since these are uniquely the benchmarks of Interpol's policy and activity. The 1963 General Assembly in Helsinki, for example, passed four resolutions; ten years later the 1972 General Assembly in Frankfurt passed twelve. In 1963 two of the resolutions concerned suppression of drugs; one concerned the identification of firearms; and one concerned the use of mass media by police in searches for missing persons—hardly more than "straight" police work in the historic sense.

In 1972 there were again two resolutions on suppression of drugs, and there was one on development of accurate drug statistics. But there also were resolutions on economic crimes, on thefts of paintings and cultural property, on counterfeiting, and on automobile theft. There were two resolutions on airline hijacking, one on traffic in firearms, and one on the suppression of slavery.

All of this suggests that Interpol faces many more problems than it did before. From the layman's point of view, this may seem disquieting, for most of us continue to hope that the world's ills are being brought under control.

The myth of the superdetective will probably always be with us. He fills an emotional need, for most people would like to believe that the wrongdoer gets his just deserts. As long as the television and movie cameras turn and comic book presses roll, there are likely to be updated versions of James Bond and Superman. In popular superdetective fiction, a serious or menacing situation is created by lawbreakers until the hero arrives and takes care of the problem by direct action that is manifestly absurd.

The means are often quite credible, however, in an age of electronics, rocket travel, infrared photography, and machines and chemicals capable of making people tell the truth. The absurdity lies in the basic concept of an individual who goes about righting wrongs without lawful authority. Audiences are willing to suspend disbelief for a man capable of stopping a criminal by superhuman means. They do not need to suspend disbelief, however, over a dramatic hero who carries out his undoubtedly good intentions without regard to the laws of the land and its system of criminal justice. In fact, audiences are not aware that such an absurdity exists, and in the fun and excitement generated by the superdetective only a spoilsport would raise this dreary issue.

Popular incredulity is more likely to be aroused by supercriminals. The idea of a lawbreaker committing one or a series of crimes, even big ones, is readily understood. And most citizens can understand the idea of a fugitive from justice fleeing the country to get beyond the reach of the law. The idea of a large-scale business enterprise constructed on criminality, however, is not so readily understood.

The public can understand the work of Interpol as it helps the police of one nation regain custody of a criminal who has jumped the frontier or as it helps police of a country to pierce the anonymity of a foreign lawbreaker. In modern times, however, criminality has taken on an entirely new dimension. Of course there are still such schemes as the Great Train Robbery in England—a most impressive enterprise of planning and organization, though decidedly old-fashioned. The modern style is crime that simulates conventional behavior and uses the patterns of business, tourism, banking, international trade, and the mass marketing of consumer products.

It might be said that this sort of crime is "invisible." The means by which a bit of white powder in a little cellophane envelope sold on the streets of Chicago gets there from its point of origin on a poppy farm in the mountain highlands of Turkey may seem invisible, but it is no more so than the means by which a tankful of gasoline in a citizen's auto in Boston gets there from a hole in the ground in Saudi Arabia.

We have taken it on faith that the advances of modern science, technology, and social organization are inherently beneficial, constructed to make life more comfortable, more affluent, more capable of fulfilling society's purposes. The bridge between these advances and beneficial effects requires managing and system in the transport of goods, operation of airlines and other conveyances, banking, investing, and so on.

The record shows that there are now criminals who find ways to operate within the established system and systematically divert a portion of its profits for their own interest. They do not go in with a gun and run away with money, gold, diamonds, paintings, a tanker of oil, or a carload of television sets. Their methods of operating parallel the normal procedures for conducting the world's work.

They open bank accounts, deposit checks, cash traveler's checks, sign credit cards, buy and sell such things as drugs, gold, diamonds, cigarettes, whiskey, corporate securities, and printshop money. They also let the old-style crook work for them, stealing on order such items as automobiles, raw diamonds, radios, tape recorders, and perfumes; or they offer the free-lancer an outlet for his loot. Noting the enormous increase in travel, they find ways to employ travelers as couriers.

In this new era of criminality, new means of exerting control over it must be devised. Historic law enforcement is geared to combat a different kind of crime, the violation of laws written by cities, provinces or states, and nations. Built into this is the dilemma of local authority and national sovereignty, in the pattern of which the modern criminal builds his immunity. To break this immunity without destroying the rights and privileges of all citizens is the challenge of our times.

Half a century ago, before the outlines of the present situation were more than dimly perceived, a group of policemen devised an organization called Interpol, an organization that has the capabilities for becoming the institution through which, uniquely, society can meet that challenge.

Index

214

216   *Index*